Relationship Selling
Achieve Everything You Deserve

Robert Spence

Cover Design by Connor Buckley

Copyright © 2017 Robert Spence

All Rights Reserved

ISBN - 13: 978 - 1542465830
ISBN - 10: 1542465834

For Jacob and Alice

My main motivation. My life. My world.
Without your love, I wouldn't have found the words to fill these pages.

I love you.

Contents

Victory belongs to the most persevering - Napoleon Bonaparte

Preface - 6

About The Author - 8

Know Your Trade - 10

Tell Me Your Goals - 14

Who Do you Surround Yourself With? - 22

The Art Of Relationship Selling - 28

You Keep Being Rejected? Good! - 46

Your Worst Enemy? You! - 54

Improve Your Personal Brand - 60

The Tennis Ball Theory - 71

Ripples In The Lake - 76

Your Competition Can Be Your Ally! - 85

You Made The Sale? Don't Quit Just Yet! - 91

Final Thoughts - 97

Your Next 30 Days - 99

Acknowledgments - 110

Further Reading - 111

Preface

You don't close a sale; you open a relationship if you want to build a long term, successful enterprise - Patricia Fripp

The role of the sales person is changing.

I believe sales professionals in the past have been viewed as snakes, ready to pounce on the unsuspecting victim, and saying whatever needs to be said to ensure a contract is signed, or a purchase is made. We all hear these horror stories of 'double glazing sales people' (sorry, not meaning to use you guys as a scapegoat here!), where these people pray on the older generation, apply gentle pressure and use scare tactics to close the deal. I am sure you know the type of person I am describing!

However now I am starting to see a change, and I am sure you are too. Sales professionals up and down the Country are starting to recognise their true role in the economy. Their role is not to just close a sale, to just take the glory and walk away with thousands of pounds of commission. The sales professional in this day and age must learn their business inside and out. Be contactable at any hour of the day to answer questions and to more or less be more of an advisor to the client. You must become the greatest person available to the client - to some degree, you must sell yourself first before you sell the product. A sales professional's personal brand is vital to the process and all of us must develop more consultancy skills to keep up with the moving times.

This is a view shared by leading sales author Jeffrey Gitomer who says that "To be the best salesperson, first you must be the best person". This statement means so much and highlights the point I am trying to purvey; if you are a great person, understand what you are selling and understand the audience you are selling to, you will naturally become a great sales person.

Looking at my bookshelf as I write this, I see countless amounts of sales books which I have purchased and read, and there are hundreds, if not thousands of books out on the market which tell us all the best way to sell and become the best in our industries; so what makes this book different? Well I, like you, am still learning. I am still developing my trade and I want to share that journey with you. I will never class myself as an expert in the field, nor will I ever look above you and preach the best way to do your job. From all of the books I have read, I have taken in every thing that I have needed to progress my learning. This book is me simply sharing everything I have read, studied and observed. I still revisit the books I have read from time to time and I hope you too can do the same with this book.

It's time to switch your mindset; stop thinking of selling as just a job. Just a job you fell in to and seem to be good at. Why are you good at it? I want you to break down every sale you have made, think of every customer or client who constantly comes back to you. Why do they buy from you? Of all the people in the world, what makes you so special? Think of sales as a trade, no similar to that of a plumber. When a person becomes a plumber, he or she starts learning from day one to become qualified. They attend courses, take lessons, read manuals and most importantly practice their skills. Once qualified, does the learning stop? Of course not! The training carries on; new technologies are released, new tools arrive on the market, and new challenges suddenly appear. This is the same for a sales person. When you got in to your sales role, were you coached, or were you given a robotic speech to memorise? How long ago did you get in to your trade? When was the last time you updated your skills and practiced a new way of thinking that had been taught to you?

Picking up this book, reading it, and revisiting it shows me you are eager to learn; just like I.

About the Author

Live in the now. Your past and future depend on it - Rob Spence

I am a sales man. No, actually let me rephrase that. I am a man. I am a man who has a passion for helping people. A passion for problem solving. A passion, and a thirst for knowledge.

My father was a sales man, a furniture sales man (a damn good one too!) and I think he is one of my early influences. I remember seeing him heading off to work wearing a nice suit, a tie, smelling of Old Spice (or some other over powering manly aftershave) and with a smile on his face. I think it was those early images that always led me to think I too would be 'suiting up' and heading out in to the big world.

I remember my first ever sales job. I was 16 and working at a local garden centre. It was Christmas time and the biggest trade was real Christmas Trees. Our job was to help families choose a tree, trim them up if needed, wrap them up in netting and take them to the customer's car. It was cold work and hard graft but I loved it. One day, one of the managers set us a challenge. We had plenty of stock of colourful, glittery metal christmas tree holders that held the real christmas trees once they had been cut. These holders retailed at £20 each, which was nearly the same asking price as a christmas tree. The challenge was set to 6 of us; who could sell the most holders in a weekend with the winner getting a crisp £20 note (not a massive commission I know, but bare in mind I was 16 - this was a sensational amount of cash!!) Challenge accepted. I took the bull by the horns and every family whom bought a tree from me were informed about the holders. It was not rocket science - I just told the families why it would make their life so much easier - It would hold the tree straight, it could hold just over a pint of water (which a tree can drink on a daily basis, just so you know) and the stand would last around 5-6 years. By the end of the weekend, I was the winner by far. That £20 commission was spent within minutes I am sure! Do you know what truly inspired me that day? It wasn't necessarily the money, and it wasn't just the thought of being the winner - it was the fact I truly felt I was helping these families and giving them something they needed. I think this attitude and this mindset rubbed off on the families, and instead of seeing some spotty teenager trying to make some quick cash, they saw a guy genuinely helping them.

I met up with one of the managers who set me the challenge recently, and he told me that the year I have described was their most successful year in terms of sales on the christmas tree stands!

After a short stint in the Police force, I started work for a fine food supplier, simply order picking and warehouse work - a bit of a career change I guess. However within 3 years, and 3 promotions I made it back to the Sales Office. I was a telesales team member, taking orders over the phone and up-selling promotional items and specials where I could.

However once again within 6 months of this role I truly found my feet in sales - sales were up by 20%, customer satisfaction and confidence was growing and my reputation within the company was on the rise. Just last month (February 2016) our year on year sales were up by 36% - other depots selling the same produce as us and running much larger operations were only up on average 2-3%.

As I write this, I am still in the Sales Office of this company, working as a sales manager, coaching and assisting our other depots, and continuing to be the best person I can be.

Know your Trade

You don't have to be great to start, but you have to start to be great - Zig Ziglar

I talk to a lot of people, and when I tell people about my passion (my career) they say "Ooh I could never work in sales" or "I don't think I am cut out for sales" and I always have to ask why! The answers as you can imagine differ from person from person, however for the majority the basis of their comments comes from their image of sales men - that stereotype I mentioned in the introduction. The pushy guy who won't take "no" for an answer. Or, their view is that they believe they would not be cut out for a high pressure sales room, taking heat from senior management and fighting for daily targets. And I understand that. For some, target driven work is terrifying and is their worst nightmare. Many people are happy to rock up to work, clock in, do the minimum required and then clock out. I don't know about you, but the thought of that depresses me! I am hoping that the fact you are reading this means you too want to strive for more.

No matter what image people have of sales people, you should always be proud of what you do for a living. Without us foot soldiers, the economic world as we know it would stop spinning.

Have you ever driven down the motorway and looked at all of the new housing developments being built? Or maybe all the business parks that are springing up? It was a sales man that was responsible for those. Every building along the motorway has been bought by a purchaser whom was advised by a sales person. Every car driving along the road right now has been recommended by a sales person no different to you or I.

I want you to truly believe in what you do. I want you to truly believe in what you sell. If you don't, I advise you to start looking for another job. I don't care what you sell. You sell - and you should be proud of that. Not too long ago I was speaking to a lady in a bar and during the conversation we started talking about what we did for a living. I asked her, "So what is it you do?" and she replied "I'm a Sales Advisor for (insert name of a large DIY retail store here)" but the way in which she said it suggested to me she was ashamed of her work. Her facial expression changed and her tone made me feel as if she was embarrassed. I said to her, "That's amazing! I'm in sales too - do you enjoy what you do?" Her response: "Yeah I guess, but I only sell screws for a living" and then laughed away her embarrassment. I couldn't quite believe this. We all spend a lot of time at work - why do something you are not entirely happy with!? To be fair, for all I know, she actually enjoyed her work and was just embarrassed to admit it. At this point I took her by the hand and said to her, "Look around you - this whole building is held together with screws, plaster, nails and bricks. Without the items you sell, this building would not be here. And if the building wasn't here, you and I would not be sharing a drink together."

If you are a veteran sales person reading this book as a bit of revision, I don't have to explain to you how varied the role of a sales person is, or how different each day can be for all of us in each industry we work in.

To you readers whom are starting a career in sales and are starting your learning journey, then I have to say - well done. I think the sales world is filled with people who fall in to sales accidentally, with no real idea of what it takes to succeed. They pick up bad techniques from their 'Sales Managers' and just wing it a little. The reason I am saying well done (you know what - well done to you veterans too!) is that you already recognise that the sales role is no different to any trade in the world. To become a doctor you must undertake years of learning, training, lectures and hands on training. Even after a Doctor graduates, he or she must stay on top of medical journals and continue their development or they will fall behind. The same ethos must be put forward to us sales people too; if you are serious about selling (and I don't mean just to make lots of commission and get rich fast - because that is not going to happen. Sorry to be the bearer of bad news!), if you are serious about a career in sales then you must learn, develop yourself, practise what you have learnt, develop your skills some more, seek advice from peers and continue your learning until the day you hang up your pen and paper and retire.

Every great company, every company whom has ever succeeded has always had a great sales and marketing team situated at the heart of it. You could have invented the worlds most economic super car that boasts 100mpg, but without a highly trained team (like yourself I hope!) the likely hood is that the product will either struggle to sell, or will take a while to kick off. As I mentioned before, gaining people's trust, building relationships and even asking for a sale (I will come to these skills later on) is what we are trained to do. Let the inventors invent, and let the transport team dispatch the item; let us advise and allow the customer to buy.

I am big fan of the Canadian Author Jules Marcoux, and in his book The Marketing Blueprint he writes, "I often hear that marketing and sales are different aspects of business...I believe they belong together, in what I call the Growth Department". The modern sales man must understand this 100% and be committed to growth for their company. I hope with working in this trade you have a bit of an entrepreneurial edge about you. By this, I guess I am trying to encourage you to engage the problem solving part of you. That part of you that finds new ways to engage with the market. I hope you are willing to first of all 'Market" the product (or maybe even market yourself!) and then "Sell" the product (or close the sale).

Never under estimate the importance of your role. You are the link. The bridge. The advisor. The friend. The consultant. In some terms you are the face of the company. If you are field sales based I imagine you are the first person your customer calls when something goes wrong, or they need that emergency delivery of important parts. If that is the case - good! You are doing everything right! If the thought of customers calling you 24 hours a day upsets you, you may need to address what your goals are in life! Having a customer call you in the hunt for a solution to a problem I feel should be seen as a massive compliment. The customer trusts you, has faith in you and believes you can help them.

In my experience, the more you see yourself as an entrepreneur, the more you will succeed in sales. Maybe even act as though you are a franchise of the company you work for. The more you take responsibility for your own work, mistakes that may be made, and the closing of sales, the more commission you will earn.

Tell Me Your Goals

Setting goals is the first step in turning the invisible into the visible - Tony Robbins

On average, I read around 1 book a week. I focus my reading on sales books, 'self help books', psychology books and other general non-fiction books that I feel will benefit my career and make me more successful. The more I study however, the more the same theories and the same practices keep cropping up. There is a lot of evidence to suggest that people whom we deem to be successful all follow the same simple rules. For me, the fact I keep reading about the same subjects is not a bad thing whatsoever! It just proves one thing; the secret to doing well in life is not such a secret after all. The problem is that these secrets just aren't taught in main stream media. They aren't on the school syllabus which is a crying shame, and they don't crop up on social media as often as I would love to see them do.

One of these secrets is so simple, and so obvious its laughable really! Nearly every successful business person or leader has put their success down to one thing; Goals.

How many times have you said to yourself, 'Oh I wish I had that car', or , 'One day I am going to own that large house over in the countryside' or even just a broad wish as 'I wish I was rich'. Have you ever said any of those things? Maybe you know of someone who says these things and then never acts upon them. They surround themselves with endless excuses for why they won't ever make it and say negative comments such as 'Oh I will never achieve that' or 'If only my parents were rich' etc etc blah blah blah. If you are one of these people, please read the below statement;

STOP!!

Stop dreaming. Stop hating everyone else for the decisions you make in your life. Stop wishing for things you can so easily have if you only worked towards them! They key to obtaining anything in life is to stop dreaming, and to start planning.

I mean it. Take the word 'dream' out of your vocabulary. Take 'wish' out of it too - if you own a dictionary I want you to literally take a pair of scissors and remove both of these words from the book! We can all dream, we can all wish, however the difference in just wanting these items of luxury and actually deserving them is how we set our targets.

We can all go through life wishing, wanting and walking around without purpose however imagine how successful your personal life would be if you planned out certain aspects? Imagine in fact how more successful your career would be if you set your own targets. Imagine yourself, before making the sales call telling yourself "I am not going to end this call without a sale" and then thinking and writing down the steps as to how you are going to achieve that.

The key to getting everything you want in life, is to write the goal down on paper. I want you take a moment, two moments if you wish, and think about what you want to achieve. What do you want to own? Is there a new car you would love to have sitting on your driveway? Maybe there is a new phone on the market that would be a massive upgrade for you. Or maybe you would love to treat your children and family to a life changing holiday. Or maybe you just simply would like to earn more money? Whatever it is, write it down below;

_____

Great, we now know what we are working towards. But to me, and to the secrets of success, this isn't quite good enough just yet. My fault really, I haven't fully written down the full instructions yet, but I just wanted to get your mind warmed up and to start you thinking.

How specific was your goal? If you just wrote down something along the lines of 'I want to get rich' or 'holiday' or 'I want a new car', then we really need to work on this a little further. I want you to think back to your goal and be fully specific about what you would like. You don't just want a new car do you? You want that amazing German make with the super awesome engine and the built in satnav and an incredible MPG record, don't you? You don't just want a holiday do you? You want to take your family to Santorini for 7 nights, in the middle of September. You don't just want to earn more money do you? If I hunted you down, and gave you £10, that would mean you have earned more money wouldn't it? But we both know that's not what you need. So what I would like you to do is sit down, think about your goal. Picture your goal. Imagine it deep within your mind. Research it. Look at photos of the item you desire. Imagine how much better your life would be in achieving it and how it will improve your lifestyle. Now write down your new goal and be so specific if I was to look at your copy of this book I would be able to replicate your goal with ease;

_____

How fun was that?! Now your plan is on paper do you feel a bit better? A bit lighter maybe? More relieved? It's funny how writing down goals can change the whole concept on our targets and make them so much more easier to reach.

Now, let's set a time scale. When do you want to hit your target? Be realistic here - you're not going to become a millionaire overnight (sorry to burst your hopes) and owning a new car in 20 years time may be a little stretched. So, now, write down realistically when you would like to hit your target;

_____

We are starting to break this down now! Let's probe a little deeper now. Your target, your goal, what do you know about it? How much does it cost? Who else owns one? Say your target is career based, have you spoken to colleagues, your bosses, your peers to see how to achieve that new promotion? That pay rise? I want you to really research your goal now and find out everything about it. Take your time here - what will it take for you to reach that target?

Hopefully, just in writing your goal down and planning it out will make the goal seem much more achievable. A lot of people I have spoken to, and learnt from, will put this target in key places around their house to keep the thought in their mind. Try it; write down your goal and put it on the bathroom mirror, or in your wardrobe maybe? Keep reminding yourself of this goal and encourage yourself to be focused on it at all times! Why not find a photo of the object you desire, print it off and use that as a visual guide?

The art of visualisation is such an incredible tool and you should really start to practise it and learn how to utilise it. I want you to start to really picture yourself achieving the goal you have written down. Take the time to picture it, live it and feel it within you. Seriously, there is no greater tool than visualising the end result! We have all heard of the famous actor, Jim Carrey. The guy to me is a comedy genius and an incredible actor. I have literally seen every movie he has ever been in and if I am honest, if ever a movie comes out with him in I trust that the movie will be good. I have such fond memories of sitting down with the family to watch his movies and I even wanted to become a Pet Detective myself for a while (and that was only 3 years ago!). Well did you know that the art of visualisation, and even writing down his goals got him to where he is today? Jim Carrey himself admits to reading self help guides during the early stages of his career. In 1995, and struggling to make a name for himself, Jim sat in his car overlooking the Hollywood Hills and wrote himself a cheque for $10million for acting services rendered and dated it for 10 years time. Jim put the cheque in his wallet and for years it sat there and deteriorated, however was always there as a constant reminder of what he set out to achieve. Nearly 10 years to the day after writing the cheque, Jim Carrey finally made it; his earnings from films Ace Ventura; Pet Detective and Dumb and Dumber earned him in excess of $10million. How incredible is that? The more I hear this story (and there is in fact a famous interview with Oprah Winfrey in which he describes this event which you should hunt down and watch), the more I feel so inspired by the art of goal setting and visualisation! Imagine if Jim had just given up in that moment amongst the hills of Hollywood, or maybe just not written that cheque, where would he be now?

One thing that has really helped me in the past couple of years, is to break goals down in to smaller steps. Sometimes, looking at a large target can really put people off (me included) and in fact can scare some people. So breaking down targets just creates smaller bitesize targets which seem so much more manageable. Think of it as like building a wall maybe; a wall is built brick by brick. Step by step, a goal can be achieved. It just breaks the whole process down. Look at the next example;

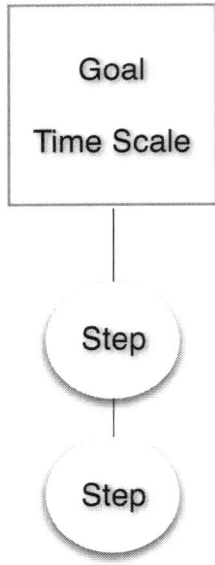

Seems simple doesn't it? And that's because it is! None of this is hard, it is so simple I have kicked myself for not setting strong targets sooner! Writing this book has been a challenge for me. I have battled self belief, procrastinated, doubted my abilities and put it off for months. It just seemed like a massive task. I have never written before, so where do I begin?! Well let's put my own goal setting theory into practice. Let me set up a goal in the exact same format as I have just advised you to do;

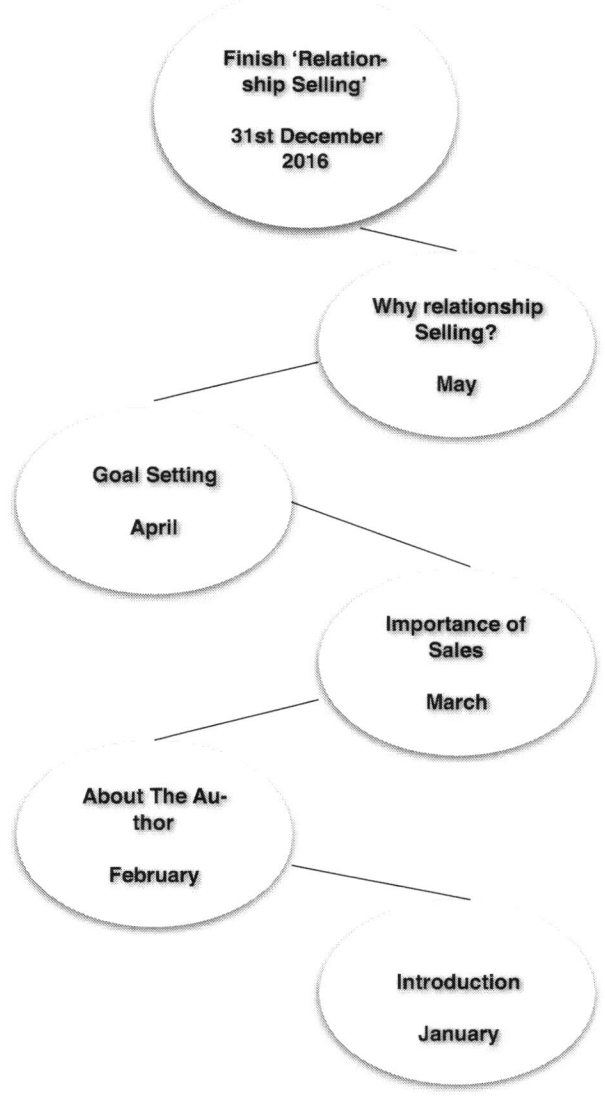

I understand it isn't a full format and is a little scarce, however I hope from that example you can see how easy a goal can seem when broken down in to smaller steps! I have set out the main target which was to complete the book. Then, just by setting monthly targets to complete the chapters the task suddenly became so much easier and manageable. The thought of writing a book can seem so daunting, and has been to me! However writing a chapter a month seems less scary!

I really want you to do that with your target! If you want a new car, go and test drive it. How much will it cost you monthly to own? Can you afford it? If not, what can you do to make sure you can afford it?

Every night before bed, I need you to start getting into the habit of planning ahead to your next day. I once read about how important our subconscious mind is, and how training it as such can help us achieve any goal we set. This is a theme I seem to pick up in many books, and the proof behind it seems so unreal, and so incredible it is such a wonder why we aren't taught it from a young age. What I have learned, is that when goals are set at night, and we visualise the goals being achieved, then at night whilst we are snoring away our mind goes into hyperdrive and starts to formulate a plan as to how it can be achieved. Step by step you will get closer to finalising your goal just by sleeping!

So at night before you go to bed - I want to you to change your routine slightly. I want you to put down your smart phone. I want you to turn the TV off. You need to read the above goals you have written. Look at the goals and visualise yourself achieving them. You do not need to go full meditation on me here, but you need to imagine yourself running across that finish line. I want you to picture yourself walking across that warm sandy beach as the surf gently rolls over your toes. Dig deep into your mind and truly feel yourself achieving your goals. Start to break the goal down and think of every step you need to fulfil to absolutely smash that goal. I assure you that as soon as you close your eyes and you doze off, your mind will work behind the scenes. Your subconscious will start to take over and ensure what you are planning will come true. It isn't some kind of voodoo magic, it is simply YOU giving YOU what you truly desire. Sometimes when people try this, the next day, or maybe after several days of practise they will hit a 'eureka' moment or come across a break that normally would be labelled as fate. However I guarantee that this is the reward for training your mind to visualise, plan and then deliver your goal for you. Try it tonight. Then try it again tomorrow. For the next 30 days. Before you sleep, in your mind, hit your goal.

Why am I telling you all of this?

The most successful sales people I have ever met have set their own targets in life. They have said to themselves that they are going to be the highest earner in their company and then use that money as a way to boost their personal life. They've said to themselves that they're not just going to mull through life; waking up, driving to work to sit at a desk all day and just slowly die a little each day! They aren't going to sit in a cubicle and do the absolute minimum work they can get away with, and then get home and wish they had more money! They have made the conscious decision to be the absolute best they can be!

I truly believe that if you read this book from back to front and implement at least 80% of what I have written, your sales will naturally increase within 30 days. What better target than that?! Using the above format (you already have a time scale set for you!!) make the goal more specific. What percentage increase in sales would you consider successful? 1%? No, that's too small! 5%? 10%? 20% maybe??

Write it down.

Now, 30 days from now you have a target - you are going to increase your sales (and increase your commission!). How are you going to do that? Keep reading......

Who do you surround yourself with?

Mentoring is a brain to pick, an ear to listen, and a push in the right direction - John C. Crosby

Before we start to look at the art of Relationship Selling and other techniques that I know will boost your sales, I want to delve deeper into you. I want to understand what makes you tick. We have already discussed your goals, and I am positive you have written down your goal and put it somewhere prominent (If you haven't, make sure you do it NOW!)

I now want to know who you look up to. Who guides you? Who inspires you? Do you have a mentor?

The more I have studied the attributes and habits of people we would consider to be successful, the more I have learnt that those with great wealth all surround themselves with like minded people to learn from, to be guided and to be supported in whatever line of work they come from.

I personally have 4 mentors whom I check in with regularly with. These four people are so inspiring and to be brutally honest without these people I would not be writing these words right now. They all come from different sales backgrounds and in my career they have truly been so invaluable in terms of their expertise and what they have been able to teach me. They may not have known it straight away, but I set myself the challenge to speak with them more, check in more often and to even go out for dinner with them. Although this was a nice chance to socialise and eat nice food, it was so important to learn about what made them tick and to ask their advice on what I needed to improve on and what goals I should be setting. I made myself a sponge (not literally of course, that would have been a bit odd), but I absorbed every ounce of positive energy they had, and listened with intent to all they could teach me. I thank them as often as I can for their guidance and I will always be so grateful for their help and patience.

Even when in social gatherings, I will always hunt down the professionals in the group. The business women. The sales professionals. I will always open them up and ask them as many questions as possible. Why? Because once again I want to learn as much as I can and I found that people love to talk about themselves and their lives. So by buying someone a drink and asking them about their career was quite a straightforward task to complete. I now have a list of contacts whom I can call upon to ask their advice.

Even Jeffrey Gitomer, one of the world's leading sales trainers tells us to "Have the right associations. Hang around the right people. Other successful people" and I can assure you that this kind of advice is mirrored by so many incredible writers and trainers!

Who would you consider to be your mentor? Your sales manager; when was the last time you offered to take them out for lunch? Or even just spent time with them in the staff room for a coffee? Even your colleagues or peers can be considered as mentors - just because they are on the same level as you does not mean their knowledge and wisdom cannot be of use to you!

I want to set you a challenge now. Similar to your goal. I want you to take the time to write down the names of three people you could consider to be mentors. Three people whom you know will be willing to assist you and guide you. Three people whom would be more than happy to check in with you from time to time to make sure you are fulfilling your true potential. Try to get three mentors from three different sectors or industries to broaden your knowledge. They can be from any walk of life but must bring to you some kind of expertise that you feel your career could benefit from.

1) _____

2) _____

3) _____

Now you have identified your mentors, I want you to reach out to them. Put this book down (not for too long though please!) and call the above people. Invite them for dinner. Take them for a coffee, or even just offer to play a round of golf with them. Anything! Just reach out, and ask to spend time with them.

Using your new found love of goal setting, make sure you set a date and stick to it!

When your mentor date comes round, make sure you use the time wisely. Of course, ask as many questions as possible. Learn about their lives, their careers and their goals. Also do not be afraid to ask them for their advice; ask them what they think about you (maybe have some wine first?) and ask them to be honest in their feedback about you. Make sure you ask if they are willing to be your mentor too! I am positive they would feel very flattered to have been asked by you, so don't be shy! But check first.

The magic of mentorship can be a two way journey also! Maybe your mentor too is looking for someone to assist them, and guide them and impart some wisdom to them. This is such an incredible honour to be a part of and I truly hope this happens for you. Life is not a sprint in which there can only be one winner. It is a marathon in which I would love to see us all win and be successful. Be willing to help out others, and be sure to give back! Be a mentor yourself to anyone willing to want you! No matter what part of your career you are in, you could have started today, or been in the sales industry for 10 years; we all have wisdom that the person on the next desk doesn't have. Be willing to help others and be willing to be at the end of the phone for anyone that needs you. Honestly there is no greater pleasure in life than helping another colleague. Make it your mission to be accessible to your peers and I assure you, you will be well compensated for your time.

In reading this, I truly hope you and I too can connect and be mentors for one another. I am sure there is so much I can learn from you, and I hope there is something I can assist you with! Please head over to robertspence.co.uk and stay in touch!

Whilst we are on the subject of mentors and positive relationships, I want to briefly flag up how destructive negative people in your life can be. There will always be people in your life who will want to put you down. Why? Because their life is boring and is failing. What is easier for these people; improve themselves, or take you down a peg? Unfortunately, the likelihood is the latter! Even in buying this book, there will be people out there who label you a nerd, a geek, or will maybe even try to discredit me in some way and say that buying this kind of book is a waste of time! I can guarantee that you do not need that kind of person in your life. They could be a relation, a friend, a colleague or simply a neighbour. My advice to you is to ditch that person as best you can. The more you can focus on positive relationships the better your career will be. Do not waste your time or your energy on these muppets that have nothing better to do than to poison you with their negativity. Listen, I am a realist, these people might be close to you and you simply cannot get away from them. They could work in your office or may even be your parents! If that is the case, just take the higher road! Listen to what this person has to say - but DO NOT take anything in! Let it go in one ear and out the other! Then, once they have shut up and quit their moaning - get out their and prove to them how incredible you are! I am sure once you pull up outside of their house in the latest Audi model they will soon eat their own words (and ask you for advice too!)

I have just finished reading Napoleon Hill's best seller Think and Grow Rich and although this book was written in 1937, there is a lot of knowledge in there that we can pass on to the modern day and we should not disregard what Napoleon has to say. In this incredible book, we learn that negative minds tried to convince Thomas A

Edison that he could not build a machine that would record a human voice and then reproduce it simply because it had never been built before. One of the most popular cars on the British roads right now is the Ford. You can't drive anywhere without noticing several Focus, Fiesta or Mondeo models! I am a proud driver of a Ford Focus right now too might I add! Anyway, Henry Ford tried out his first Automobile on the streets of Detroit and many negative people told him that no one would pay money for such an invention! And now take a look around you! Henry Ford in that moment could have agreed with these losers, but he believed in himself! He kept going, kept moving forward, kept setting goal after goal until eventually his dream was realised! By doing so he not only received great recognition and built such an incredible wealth that I am sure he enjoyed spending every single penny on endless projects, (I can picture him building a car in his garage simply out of boredom!) but he also fulfilled his dream - no, not his dream. His GOAL!

If you study legends such as these, the more you will see that they surrounded themselves with positive mentors whom did everything they could to help and grow together as a team.

Go back and revisit the goals you have set in the previous chapter. Read them aloud. Think of every person you consider close to you; if you can truly imagine any of these people mocking you, doubting you or questioning your ability to complete them then I am so happy to say that it is that person you need to get rid of. I know it is hard, and will not come easy. Very recently I have limited my contact with a person whom I have considered a friend since the age of 8. However the amount of negative energy I have had to repel from him was unreal and I want you to truly believe the words I am writing. If I can ditch these negative influences, then you can too.

I really don't want to end this chapter on a negative note. I am not a negative person and so I feel a few words on a positive note will revert our mindset a little before we move on! For the past couple of days I have been working closely with colleagues, assisting their sales teams and motivating them. I became a mentor to three new people which I am so excited about! I have already had emails from them telling me about the positive results they have had so far and I cannot wait to see what is to come from them! Just to see these colleagues responding so positively is what our job is all about. These are people whom I now can't wait to meet up with again and I cannot start to explain how proud of them I am and how excited I am to see our relationships grow and develop!

Now, let's get back on track. Relationship Selling.....

The Art Of Relationship Selling

A business that makes nothing but money is a poor business - Henry Ford

Several years ago I took the plunge and entered the property market. That sounds more intense than what it actually was. Basically, I bought my first house. I was a single man buying a house, and I will be fully truthful with you here; I really did not know how it all worked (to some degree I still don't!) Anyway, after some research and planning (and goal setting and visualisation of course) I found the property I loved and went on the hunt for a mortgage advisor. I am sure you have been through the same process; as soon as the market place knows you are looking for financial advice, every advisor suddenly appears and starts to call you, email you or sends you letters through the post. As this was happening, one man stood out to me; Allan. He was recommended to me (recommendations are KEY to relationship selling) and everything about him just made him stand out from the crowd. And do you know why he stood out? He genuinely listened to me, understood what I required and he helped me far beyond what I would have ever expected. Nothing was ever too much trouble. He was always contactable by text no matter what time of day or night and he even went above and beyond what a normal advisor would be expected to do. Due to all of this; I gave him my business. However, the story does not stop there. I have struck up a real bond with this man and I now use him for many of my financial needs. When it comes to personal finance, wills and insurance the first person on my mind is him. Even now I am looking to move house once again and upsize and guess who is looking after my mortgage again - Allan. From the minute I enquired about putting my house on the market, I have had every Dick, Tom and Harry contact me trying me to use their service and even trying to undercut Allan on price, however I have stuck by him 100%. I trust Allan and his decisions and I feel that moving forward I will always be able to rely on him to give me the best advice.

I am sure you too can think of sales professionals you have come across in your life who you trust and who have really helped you. I am sure you have a car mechanic you always turn to, or maybe a builder or other tradesmen that you can always rely on and trust. And this is how simple Relationship Selling is. I wish I could tell you that it is an incredible secret of the universe in which you must pass through seven levels of enlightenment to reach - however it isn't. Nice people get repeat business. And that is the fundamental basis of relationship selling.

The first sales book I ever read (and I hope too that you have read it!) is Dale Carnegie's How to Win Friends and Influence People. This book has sold way over 16 million copies worldwide, been translated into thirty six different languages and is one of the key foundations to any person wanting to build a career in sales. I even bought a copy of this book for a new member of staff that works alongside me whom had never worked in sales as I feel this should be the Bible to all new sales professionals. For those that are not aware of this golden transcript, Dale Carnegie was an early pioneer of self development and taught motivational techniques to millions. In his writing, Dale aimed to increase the readers popularity, handle complaints better, make friends quicker, become a better speaker and to increase their persuasion skills. Early on in my career this book truly shaped my way of working and rewired my mind to act differently and looking at my sales figures and how far my career has come since reading it. I would thoroughly advise any sales professional to take the time to read this book. How to win Friends and Influence People also inspired me deeper. The book taught me about relationship selling and allowed me to propagate my own ideas and techniques which I am now so proud to share with you.

A bad sales man will close the sale, and close the relationship along with it - Rob Spence

In the introduction of this book, I spoke about sales professionals whom go about things in the wrong way. Yes they can more than likely make a commission and use simple wording tactics or scare tactics to make a sale, but in doing so they are more than likely going to close the relationship at the same time - and this does not lead to further sales. You see, the key to increasing your sales is repeat business. One off sales will scratch your back for a while but the commission will eventually dry up. If you run out of recommendations, where are you going to turn to? If your reputation as a person is poor, who will want to buy from you? Your sales will dry up, your commission will dry up and you will be back at square one. In reading this book I can see that you do not want to be like that - you understand the 'long game' and understand the importance of patient selling.

There are industries out there where you may feel like you are in a one shot opportunity to close a sale, or where you feel there will be a lack of repeat custom. This could be mobile phone sales, car sales, bathroom or furnishing sales etc. You may feel that by signing a customer into a long contract will satisfy your sales quota - I can tell you now that this is not the case in the long run. Imagine yourself selling to a mother of three teenage children a brand new phone on a 24 month contract. You have handled the sale well, answered all the questions correctly however your attitude has been quite pushy. You have been so eager for this customer to sign the contract you have failed to inform her of the extra costs involved down the line, or the fact her monthly premiums will rise in 6 months, or maybe you did not give her the minimum amount of data she simply needs to run her phone efficiently. Anyway, she signs and leaves the shop with her new phone. Imagine this same customer then months later finding out she has been sold a product that she is not entirely happy with. She grows frustrated, angry and upset with you for the fact that you were dishonest. Low and behold three months later, her three teenage sons are in need of new phones. Who do you think she is going to turn to? You? I doubt it. You have gained commission on one contract (well done) but you failed to see the bigger picture and lost out on three more commission cheques in your pocket! Rewinding time a little, lets imagine you were completely honest with the customer and fulfilled every single one of her needs. She was left entirely happy with your service and even sent in to your employer a raving and glowing recommendation. Once again, her three sons are in need of new phones - who does she turn to now? That's right - YOU!

I speak to my colleagues and peers about something I call the Customer Cycle Of Satisfaction, and it discusses a chain of events which leaves every person in the chain happy. This chain includes your customer, potentially their customers too (if you are selling business to business) and how then that repeat custom comes full circle back to you. This Cycle can then be turned into a chain of Cycles dependent on recommendations and via word of mouth. The one person this benefits is you, your commission and the people you spend that money on!

The industry I work in is food sales to businesses. I know that if I sell an amazing product that can be sold on by my customer at a higher price, then I know my customer will be happy - their profits will increase which in turn improves their quality of life. I know also that if the product is so good that their customer base loves the product, then the likelihood is that their customer will come back for more! This then means repeat custom for me as the Cycle of Satisfaction continues to grow. If the business I am selling to is making money and proving to be profitable, I too will reap in these rewards.

Let's try to visualise this Customer Cycle Of Satisfaction in a little more detail:

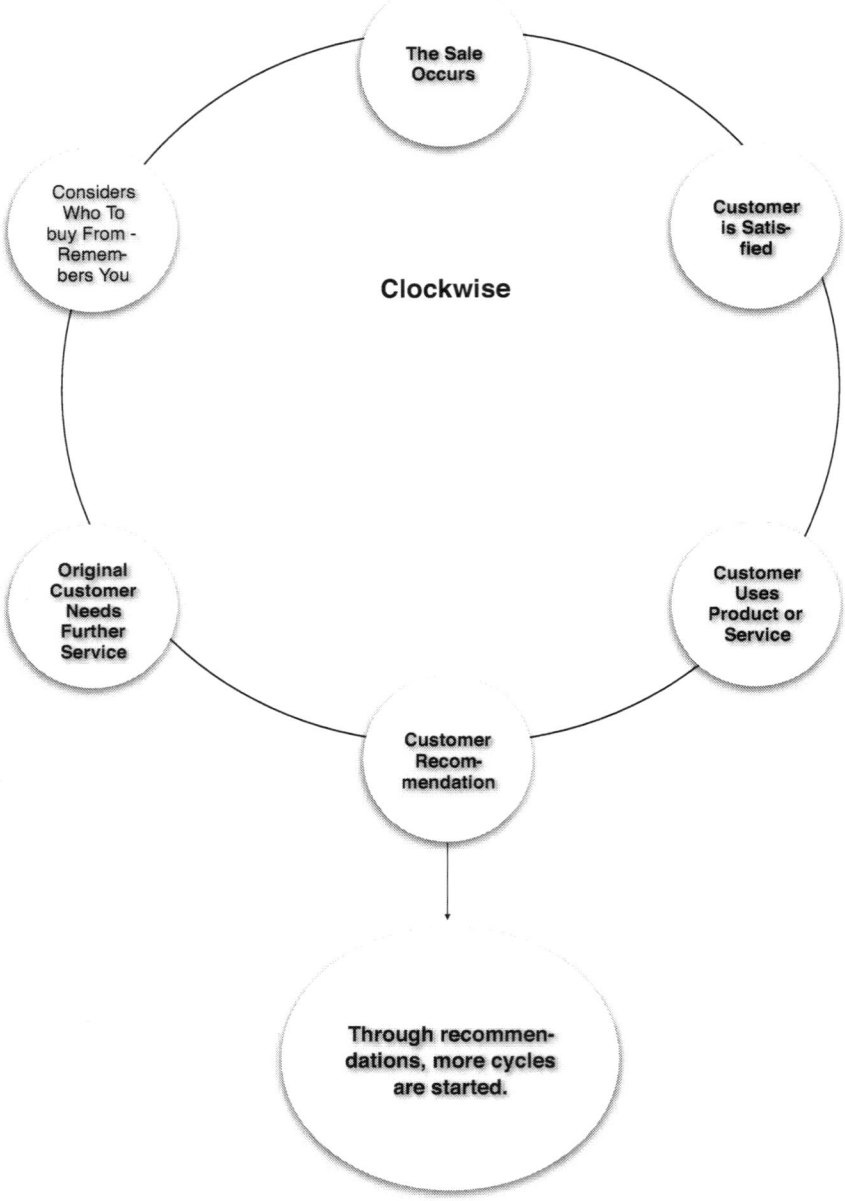

Let's start this cycle from the very top. The first section is where the sale occurs. This can start from the opening of a sale, or even from the close of a sale. To some degree, a sale does not need to close for a person to be considered a customer in which case this cycle can start from the initial pitch or the opening conversation. If you have done everything right and followed my advice the customer will be satisfied and happy with their purchase and will go on to take the product home, or will use the service within their business. Of course, the customer is happy with the product, so the good feedback is passed on to family members, friends and perhaps business associates. It is these recommendations that will do wonders for your commission pay check. From that referral, more sales can be made, and the more cycles can be introduced. Imagine if this happened to every single one of your sales - how closer would you be to achieving your goals if this happened?

Let's head back to the original cycle; your initial customer carries on using your product to the point where they need more. Or maybe they need a new unit of an item installing, or are in need of more services due to their continued business growth. With so many products on the market, who will they turn to? You!

You see, everything in our trade is linked. Everything comes back to us full circle eventually if we can all remember to be patient! I work primarily in business to business sales, so my customer's profits are very important to me. If my customers are making money and keeping their customer's happy, they will need to come back to me for more advice and more products. If my customer is succeeding, then their customer base will develop. If their customer base grows, all of a sudden more products needs to be sourced; which is where I can stand in to support, advise and supply.

Just imagine if a sale was made, and the customer wasn't happy. The cycle ends within the second circle. Or perhaps you start the sale; conversations are opened however for whatever reason the prospect isn't happy with your service or they catch on to some raw tactics and dishonesty coming from you; once again the cycle will end way before it starts.

The above very briefly illustrates how the Customer Cycle of Satisfaction works and what it can do to improve your sales. I set out with a goal at the start of this book - to increase your sales in 30 days and by studying and understanding the above cycle I know you will achieve this!

If you make a sale, you can earn a commission. If you make a friend, you can earn a fortune. - Jeffrey Gitomer

I want to delve deeper now into how we need to develop these deep relationships and how we need to maintain them. We have all made friends throughout our lifetime and building relationships with our customer's is no different. One thing I set out to achieve in my career is to become friends with those who use my services and you should do the same thing. So, where do we start?

Be Approachable and On Call

In relationship selling, you no longer work 9-5. You are on call all hours of every day. Of course, there is a limit to this and I do not want you thinking you have to take phone calls every night at 11pm disturbing your personal life. However you must make yourself accessible and contactable no matter where you are. This is so easy to do in the modern day. We all effectively walk around with tiny computers in our pockets that have so many apps on them to make us reachable in many forms. I personally use text, phone, WhatsApp, Facebook, Instagram, Email and Twitter and other apps which allow me to be contacted by my customers and colleagues at any hour of any day. This then means there is no excuse for me not being able to contact a customer, or for them to ask me questions. I have made it clear to all that buy from me that they can use me for an queries they have. I even did this in the early stages in my career where I was simply put in place to answer calls and take orders - I took that step above and gained the trust of our clients.

Always return calls. Always return messages. Even if you do not know the answer to the question, or even if you are in a position where you cannot answer. Respond to your customer and ask them to call the main office or contact a colleague - at least then you are not ignoring the request and you can lead your customer in the right direction.

Whilst we are on the topic of being accessible, I want to share with you the valuable, and sometimes overlooked advantage of your voicemail. There will be times when someone calls you and of course you cannot be reached. We all have access to our voicemails and this is something I feel is underused by many. In reading books by Jeffrey Gitomer, I learned about the importance of making our voicemail greeting welcoming, funny, different and warming. Make the person calling you WANT to talk to you again! How many times have you called someone to only be greeted by a dreary tone saying "You have reached the voicemail of Rob, please leave a message and I shall call you back". Boring!! Would I want that bore to call me back anyway?! Have some fun with your greeting. At the very least, sound excited, sound thankful that someone has taken time out of their day to contact you. My voicemail is set as "Hi, this is Rob Spence. I am probably here, I am just avoiding someone I don't like. Leave a message, and if I don't call back - It's you!" The amount of people who have left messages whilst laughing complimenting it has been unreal. Have fun with your voicemail - make it fun! Life is too short to be serious all of the time, right!?

<u>Listen</u>

Our bodies were designed with two ears and one mouth for a reason. During your conversations with your customers, how much time do you spend talking, and how much time do you spend listening? I can assure you, we can all listen more. Listening to our customers will not only give us more attempts to find solutions to their problems, but it will also help to solidify our relationships. Everyone loves the sound of their own voice and we all love to tell stories about our lives. When meeting with a prospect like this, just listen! Do not just sit there pretending to listen either whilst you are really just thinking about what you will have for lunch - actively listen. Pay attention. Ask probing questions. Really study what your client is telling you. If a client is willing to talk to you then you know they already like you, so do them a favour and listen!

Make sure you truly take in what they are saying. They could be giving you clues to what they require as a customer. If this is the case take notes, or mental notes if need be and be ready to probe later on. There could be more services you can offer this person down the line if you listen and pay attention. When I talk to my customers and they enquire about a certain ingredient, I will always ask, "What are you doing with that?". The passion for their work then opens up the customer more and they go on to tell me the dish they aim to create, and tell me more ingredients they will be using. In listening, I can then probe other items the customer could require from us which they may not have originally called for or even know I sold.

On top of listening to your customer or client's needs for products, truly listen to things they tell you about their private life too. Just asking them about their children or wives can mean so much to a client and makes them feel welcomed by you. How many times have you been to your local shop and the assistant has asked you about certain aspects of your life? I am sure it has made you feel welcome and you actually enjoy the conversation. Be sure to remember also what the client has told you. There is nothing worse than entering a conversation a week later asking how their wife is when he has never been married. If you are poor at remembering details like this, take notes! Write everything down so that before you call this customer again you can briefly return to these notes as a guide. There are plenty of books on the market, even videos readily available on Youtube which will assist you in memory skills and give you advice on how to remember facts a lot easier.

Founder of memoryschool.com, Mark Channon was once ranked third in the world as a Grand Master of Memory. In his book, Improve Your Memory, Mark discusses in great detail the most common types of memory and how memory is developed. There are plenty of 'try it now' exercises within the book which give the reader some great exercises to put in to practice. If remembering facts about your customer is at times a tough task for you, I urge you to buy Mark's book and put in to use the advice he gives! It has certainly helped me along my journey. Now, if I could only remember where I put his book...

Research

I mentioned earlier that we all carry little computers around with us in our pockets, and yet they are rarely used to their full potential. The power of the internet has allowed us to research our customers and other companies so easily and it can be done at any time of the day, and yet how many of us fail to use these tools to their full potential?

On personal selling, or selling to the general public it will be very hard to research their needs way before they approach you. This is where the importance of listening to the customer's needs comes into play. However when selling business to business, or in a market where repeat custom is key, you should be researching your customer way before first contact has been made. This is not to generally be nosey or just as an excuse to procrastinate, it is to learn about the customer's needs way before the customer brings that need to your attention.

Your first stop should be their company website. This will give you plenty of information you need on the size of the company, how many people work there, what their mission statement is, or even what their recent financial statements looked like. Even social media can be a great source of information for their latest projects, successes and events. Try even studying the companies MD on Linkedin, or other social media formats. The more you learn, the more you will be able to find ways to do business with this company. Also, you will be a step ahead of the competition in the fact that if you were to sit down with the client, and they start to tell you about the company, what their market is like and who their competitors are, you will understand it a lot faster as you have already studied this information in great detail and everything told to you should just be revision.

Do not be afraid to mention you have visited the company's website either! It can be a massive compliment to your client and will ingrain you on to their minds as someone who truly takes the time to find the right sales solutions for them. You can say things like;

"I see last week you held an event at the local Hilton - how did it all go?"
"I saw you have just redesigned your website! It looks amazing. Did it take long to complete?"
"Tell me more about the meeting you are having next week. I see online it is going to be quite popular"

In doing so I assure you that you will stand out from your competitors 100% and will give you the edge over anyone else.

Give Praise

As mentioned before, everyone loves to hear about themselves and loves to be told how well they are doing. Using the research you have conducted on the customer, never feel shy to give praise. If they have been doing well, tell them! If your customer has just signed a new contract which will guarantee millions of pounds of turnover for their company - congratulate them! Always reinforce the positives!

Something I will delve in to deeper later on is our competition and how we should deal with them. Never be afraid to praise their work too! They are competition for a reason and as I will explain later on in this book you should never bad mouth your competitor. Displaying such a negative character to a customer or client will only have a negative impact on your reputation.

If you can't say something nice, don't say nothing at all - Thumper (Bambi 1942)

Be Grateful

Thank you.

Two words that can mean the world to any person and help to solidify and strengthen a relationship. Manners cost us nothing, and should be at the top of your priorities after a sale is made.

Remember the last time you held the door open for someone and they just walked through without such a second glance back at you. How annoyed did that leave you feeling?!

You should always thank your customer for the sale. Always. After all, due to their decisions you have just made some commission, kept your boss (and family no doubt) happy and just hit your monthly target.

I am not saying to say something scripted or fake. Refrain from saying "Thank you so much for shopping with us today. Have a good day now!" or some other scripted verse a super market checkout boy has had to memorise. However be sincere in your gratitude. Simply saying "Thank you so much for your order today, we really appreciate it", or if you have taken an order following months of negotiation and trust building just saying "thank you so much for your vote in confidence" can mean so much and yet take no time at all to say.

Think of how sweeter this World would be if we were all grateful for the smaller things in life.

Be Honest

When I first started to think about writing this book, I decided I would head out for dinner with my mentors, and interview as many professionals as I could. You can see above how important research is to me and I felt if I was going to write and expect you to read this book, you would need a fountain of knowledge to dive into and come out swimming!

I took one of my mentors, Victor out for dinner one cold Autumn night just for a general catch up and to seek his advice on all things sales. Victor is a key account manager for a World leading chocolate brand and has worked within the sales industry for years! I was probing Victor on the reasons he felt his career was a success, and what he considered to be the key things which have helped him to continue to progress. I went on to ask what the number one rule was I should set myself if I was to progress my career. Victor took a sip of wine, looked me deep into my eyes, put his glass down and said "Never bullshit to anyone Rob". His tone was so sincere you could see that this was a point that Victor truly believed in. I probed him further, and the advice I was given was that the most honest of sales people are always at the top of the class. The simple reason is this; an honest sales professional will always gain repeat business, will benefit from recommendations and will always be at the top of the buyer's list of trusted advisors. Victor told me that we must never lie or distort the truth. If your company can't fulfil an order, be honest. If you cannot get your price any lower, be honest. If you feel the services your customer requires just can't be met by your company for what ever reason, be honest. Yes, in that moment you may be pushing your customer towards a competitor however I assure you that your honesty will reside well with your customer and they know that in you they have a trusted ally who will always work in an ethical way.

<u>Follow up</u>

Many sales professionals make the mistake of celebrating a sale too early. As soon as that commission hits their bank account, it's a done deal. Or maybe before that! Some people become complacent as soon as the order has been raised and that is not what Relationship Selling is about.

Relationship selling carries on for months or maybe years after the sale has been made. If you remember the Cycle of Customer Satisfaction chart in the earlier pages you will understand that the happier the customer is then the chance of you getting a repeat order in the future becomes higher!

The time in which you follow up on a sale is completely up to you and you must grasp and understand your client to know when to follow up. Some customers may want to be left alone for a while for the product or service to be settled in. They may have other projects on too which need their attention and your constant calling to ensure that the product has been delivered may just be unwelcome. You may however have a customer who needs their hands holding at every step of the way and there is nothing wrong in this at all! You are a professional, and I trust that you can grasp the relationship and understand how much you need to probe (if you have followed the steps I have outlined in earlier pages then you will definitely have an understanding as to how your customer reacts).

The follow up is an extension of showing gratitude to some degree. Of course, you want to make sure that all of the promises you have made to your customer have been fulfilled however also works as a way and an excuse to saying thank you! Maybe use the gratitude as an excuse to follow up? "Jim, I was just calling to say thank you once again for your recent order! I am so excited to hear about the benefits the product has had on your profits! How did you find the process anyway? Was the installation as pain free as I said it would?"

The follow up process may also open up sections of feedback which the customer does feel you need to improve on. If that is the case - do not brush over this! If a customer is telling you that something can be improved, listen! Take notes and probe! Not only will you then have the chance to iron out these creases for the next order you create, but you will solidify your relationship via the art of listening!

Own up To Mistakes

Have you ever studied the art of mindfulness? Or maybe even dabbled in meditation? Well, some of the early practises of these is to focus on how our bodies work and to focus on certain aspects of our anatomy. Deep breathing exercises are designed to focus us on gorgeous oxygen entering into our nose and working it's way down in to the lungs. It is in here the oxygen passes through hundreds of alveoli and exchanges with carbon dioxide coming the other way. This is all regulated by our amazing hearts which by using muscles out of our control, pump that oxygenated blood through our bodies which then allow us to move and function. The more you take the time to focus on these functions the more you realise something; We are human.

Yes, that is right, we aren't machines. We aren't robots. We are humans, and we all make mistakes!

If you do make a mistake, own up to it! Do not blame anyone else or make every excuse under the sun; this isn't year 4 of school and you are trying to persuade the teacher that your dog ate your homework! Man up, and start to find a solution to the problem! To some degree, mistakes should be celebrated. They give you the chance to be the Knight In Shining armour and allow you the chance to save the day. What better way to solidify your relationship with someone than by turning up, with the product your customer needed yesterday in the back seat of your car!

Of course we don't want mistakes to happen in the first place and this is where you need to process that feedback and ensure it doesn't happen again! If you made the mistake, look in the mirror, slap yourself and move on. If it is a company mistake don't get mad or angry. What is that going to do?! It will only drag morale down and make you look like a right muppet! Stand up, be counted, and get to the root cause of the problem. Liaise with the transport manager, warehouse manager, operations manager or whoever you can and come up with a positive plan of action to ensure this doesn't happen again.

I once took an order for a customer of ours for a large delivery of fresh meat. The customer had a huge event to cater for at the weekend and so placed the order several days before to ensure we could guarantee delivery. Of course, on the phone he was quite anxious with the order and kept emphasising the point that this was an important order. I reinforced his confidence with him, listened to his worries and reassured the weakened points he raised and I finalised the order. Well, delivery day came around and you can guess what happened. The order was not delivered! I received a call from the customer demanding to know what had happened, demanding the order be delivered that same day and was clearly angry and mighty pissed off with us - he was adamant he would never use us again for any products. I ended the call to hunt down answers. I started to investigate what had happened, and the the failing could only be put down to a system error. The error was 'live' on the system and for all intents and purposes should have been delivered, however it had not. I couldn't tell the customer this could I?! "Sorry Luke your order won't be with you because the system says no." What a rubbish excuse. I hate that kind of 'computer says no' kind of attitude. I took the decision to take responsibility for this mistake. I didn't have to, however I felt in blaming me, I would be allowed the chance to rectify the problem and regain the customer's confidence in me and our company's procedures. I called the customer up, and explained, "The mistake was all mine; I have entered the delivery date for tomorrow which is why it had not been processed. However, I have organised a special delivery for you later on today and although it is later than what we planned it will still be with you later on today". I cannot begin to tell you what a good decision this was. Although of course we failed operationally, and trust from the customer had been tested, having me take the blame and then finding a solution just solidified the relationship further. This was a customer whom I felt would after this stop calling, or at least put their orders through someone other than me but I was wrong; after this mistake the customer always called up and asked for me personally and trusted every decision I made.

Truly Care

The most sincere sales professionals always come out on top. Fact!

The more you care about your customer and how well they will succeed, the more your relationship will profit! Remember the Cycle Of Customer Satisfaction, and remember every step I have written in the pages prior to this. If you sell a product to a customer whom has no real use for it just to make yourself a quick commission you will never see that customer again - sorry, you have just lost them to your competition!

Put yourself in to the mindset of your client, or maybe even picture yourself on the company's board of Directors. If you were, would you buy the product you are trying to sell? Would it benefit you in anyway?

Care about what you are doing, and care about the decisions you are trying to influence. If you do care, I promise your sales will increase in 30 days.

Gifts

The last time you went to do your weekly food shop, were you tempted with a free sample of a new cooking sauce? Or maybe a shot of coffee? Or perhaps in the magazine you bought your wife, was there a sample of the latest perfume?

If you did, how more positively did you feel about the brand? Were you more tempted to buy that product? Studies suggest you were!

Psychologists call it the Power of Reciprocity, and in Robert B.Cialdini PH.D's book, Influence, The Psychology of Persuasion, we learn that the simple of act of a gift, or even a free sample can do wonders for your sales!
I am not suggesting to go to you all of your customers and bribe them with gifts and the latest free samples, however it should be considered a useful tool in your sales kit!

We are held by the invisible force of favours, and even the smallest of favours can lead us to reciprocate with a much larger favour in return! A gift can be exchanged as part of a thank you package for a sale, or can be sent long before you even cold call a customer. Be creative with your gifts too! If you have a customer with young kids why not buy them books signed by their favourite author? Or if they are dog lovers, buy them a gift for their dog! Make it personal. No one wants a generic bottle of champagne you send to everyone! If you have a customer who told you months ago their favourite band or singer, buy them tickets to their next show (pick yourself up a ticket too so you can solidify your relationship!) I assure you in doing so you will be more likely to pick up repeat sales than if you were to just send a generic gift.

<u>Final Say</u>

The basics of relationship selling are easy. Put simply, be nice. Be friendly and look after every single one of your prospects, customers and clients and treat them like they are loved family members. Without these relationships, and the love you put in to them, you will not have the money to fund whatever lifestyle you have set out.

Having said that, Relationship Selling is not easy. It is damn hard work! If you do not work on your relationships, they will fizzle out and a competitor will swoop in and take over. It is just like a marriage. You need to work on your relationships, work through the harder times and celebrate the good times.

Bring worth to the relationship. Check in with your ~~customers~~ friends. Make them laugh. Solve their problems. Be there, as a friend and an advisor and never forget the rules I have written to you in the past several pages.

You all have best friends. Think about the work it takes to retain that friendship and put that same amount of effort, if not more, in to your business relationships.

You Keep Being Rejected? Good!

*I've failed over and over again in my life. And that is why I succeed -
Michael Jordan*

"No. No. No."

"No thank you."

"Not today."

"I don't have the time."

"You're wasting my time. You're Wasting your time."

"I already own one."

"Please leave."

"Please stop calling us."

"No."

"I am just not interested."

You have heard all of these before, right? If you are new to sales, the above may be a first to you. If so, get used to it. The modern sales professional will go through so many rejections way before any sale ever occurs. It just comes part and parcel with the role and if you aren't ready for that you really need to get used to people hanging up on you, doors being slammed in your face and people at times being rude to you. I am not telling you this to scare you away or cause you to panic - I just want you to be ready. Not just to be able to cope with rejection but also learning how to accept rejection and being brave enough to either find a reason for the rejection, or to move on to the next prospect.

I once had a young member of staff start with us in the office who had never had any experience in sales, his customer service skills were low and he was a real project. (I must say on a side note to this, that Sam's progress has been unreal and he is a colleague I truly trust in our office and I know he has a bright future in our industry.) Anyway, when he started he could not handle rejection, at all. He took it so personally that with every rejection he took he reacted like someone had just punched his Nan in her bladder. My emphasise on Sam eventually was to start to get him to up sell products to customers; he had reached a good standard in customer service and taking orders over the phone however I needed him to switch to that next gear and start to then progress those calls and conversations in to more target based selling. I set him easy targets to get him started and ran through every technique and every tip I have included in this book. Then picture the scene; the first call comes in and he takes the order, listens to the customer's requirements and ensures their needs are met. Perfect. He would then go on to tell the customer about the item he is trying to sell. Despite Sam talking confidently on the phone and doing well to run through his pitch, the customer said no. Immediately just by listening to Sam's tone and his body language you knew what had happened. All of a sudden those barriers raised up within Sam and he did not like it. When this happened, for the rest of the day, he did not ask any other customer to buy his product. Why? Because of his FEAR of rejection! He took the rejection so personally he felt that more people would reject him and it became a vicious cycle. Of course, I took Sam to one side and explained to him everything I am telling you right now, and with a bit of practice and reinforcement Sam has truly come on as a sales professional and he can get rejected like the rest of us!

Luckily for me, I was rejected by a lot of girls during my teenage years so I am totally used to it!

If you re-read the chapter on Relationship Selling and study the points I have made about building relationships, you will limit your chances of rejection. Hopefully by building a relationship with a customer, and understanding their needs you will have offered to them a service or product that benefits them so the chance of a 'no' is reduced.

Being rejected does allow you the chance to work on yourself and learn from your mistakes. Remember none of us are perfect! If a customer says no, and rejects the product, be bold and ask the question; "Why?" The customer will generally tell you honestly tell you the reasons if they trust you. This then keeps the door open for you to argue any rejection that they may mention - this gives you another chance to sell your product once again. Just by asking the question 'why'. Don't feel like you are being rude about it - in theory you have already lost the sale so you have nothing left to lose. Why not say, "No problem at all, I understand. May I ask why you don't want to use us right now?" or "Was there anything I could have done differently to persuade you?". It is by asking questions like this that will once again open up the customer and you will get an honest as to why you failed....for now.

Your Pitch Was Not Up To Scratch

Personally, I dislike the word 'Pitch'. I don't know why. There is just something about the word that reminds me of old school selling. Giving me the image of a nervous guy with a dated Powerpoint presentation by his side, with poorly set out annotations that do nothing to inspire the buyer!

A pitch however, or whatever you wish to call it, in my eyes should be 80% questioning and listening to the customer, with the remaining 20% used to instruct the buyer by offering answers and solutions.

Just to clarify, a pitch can be ANYTHING you say or demonstrate to a customer to encourage them to buy. This can be on a shop floor of a retail store. It could be over the phone to a customer who is hundreds of miles away, or could just be a chance encounter at a networking event. Have a look at your pitch right now for one of your products or services - how much of that pitch is questioning, and how much of it is discussing?

A pitch gives you the chance to solidify your understanding of your customer's needs (remember, you have already researched the hell out of them so you know them back to front, so this is now just revision!) and then to discuss the benefits of your product and get your prospect so excited by you and your services that they want to buy! You have few chances to get this right, maybe only one. So make it fun, make it sexy. Make it stand out from the other 5 pitches the buyers have listened to that same day! I can assure you now that buyers look for more than just price - they want to buy from a trusted source and want to make sure that the money they are giving you, whether it is £10 or £10,000, is being spent wisely.

If you nail your pitch, and explain everything fully about what you have to offer, and if you answer your buyer's questions you are going to reduce the chance of them pulling out of the sale due to lack of information. That is why it is so important to ask questions there and then - get all of the buyer's doubts out in the air early on and be so confident in reassuring the doubts that by the end of the pitch there is no such thing as doubt in the atmosphere.

People hate to be sold, but they love to buy! - Jeffrey Gitomer

Price is Rarely a True Issue

If your buyer is questioning your price - you are nearly there! As soon as someone starts to haggle with you, it proves that they want the product or service you have to offer!

Price in my opinion is an obstacle you will always come across, however if you smashed your pitch it rarely will be an issue. The likelihood is that they DO want to buy, but there are some doubts deep down and the buyer is simply using price as a wall to hide the real reason for rejection.

Discounting is just an easy option for an opener - Rob Spence

If you have faith in your product and know that it is the best on the market there should be no part in you which feels you should need to discount the product. Discounting the product only makes you look like you aren't so confident in your product after all and it just devalues the product. If you could sell it cheaper, why didn't you just set the price lower in the first place?

The best way to counter this kind of rejection, or the classic line of "Is this your best price?", is to be honest and say "Yes it is. We have already priced this competitively, and due to the quality of the product I really wouldn't want to devalue it". I can't count the amount of times I have used this statement and still got the sale. It is not because I am being greedy, but I am positive that the best price has already been set and is a fair price. I am an honest person, and in this scenario you are not ripping any person off; you are simply setting a fair price for your customer, your business and of course, you too.

Always ask the buyer if this is the only reservation that they have which is putting them off from buying. As I mentioned before the buyer could be using the price issue as an excuse for deeper reasons - always ask the question and I assure you that you will get honest answers back.

There may be times when your buyer just cannot afford your product or service. If you feel this is the case, and maybe you are selling more on a personal level as opposed to business to business selling, then either try to address the pricing structure, look for finance or credit options or just be willing to accept that you aren't going to win this sale just yet.

<u>You Are Not Speaking to The Decision Maker</u>

I remember at one stage in my career, I was trying to increase the sales on a certain range of products the company I worked for stocked, and I was being absolutely relentless in my approach and would not stop calling out until I had made the personal targets I had set myself that day. I was dialling out to a customer and without me knowing, I touched a wrong number on the phone. Of course, I was calling someone completely different to who I should have been calling. I was so excited about hitting my target and selling more units, I didn't really listen to the person on the line when they answered and I assumed I was speaking to the customer I had targeted. Anyway, I went ahead with my pitch, not using my 80/20 ratio of listening to talking during my pitch and I just went full throttle about how this product was far superior to what they were currently using, how it was priced so competitively and I asked how many units I could send out to them. After a second or two of silence, the person on the other line told me who I had called. I had called a Coal Mine association who were not a customer of ours let alone would have any use for this product! What a waste of time this was! This is why listening is vital.

The pitch I used I am sure was absolutely spot on. I am sure I had spoken about every benefit this product had, how it would improve the customer's profits etc, but what I failed to do was speak to the decision maker and I failed to listen and confirm the customer's needs!

How many times have you failed to identify the right decision maker and wasted your time on a pitch only to be told that they need to seek advice from their manager? I am sure moving forward with your new passion for researching your customers way before you talk to them, this won't happen often; But it does happen more often than you think!

If this is the case, don't panic! You can use this to your advantage. The key is to not lose faith and do not seem annoyed - this person you have been talking to can be your assistant in selling the item and most of the time can sell the product on your behalf and normally way better than you ever can! You will need to ask them who you need to speak to, and see if you can meet with them right away. If not, arrange a meeting and ensure that your first point of contact sits in on the meeting too. Remember, this person has said that he needs to clear it with his manager - if he was not interested or felt that the company had no use for your product or service he would have told you. Get him on board, win him over - and go and target the true decision maker!

The Buyer is in a Bad Mood

This is something I think we can all forget - the buyer too is human, they have emotions and may not be in the right frame of mind when you meet with them.

This is the point I have had to get across to Sam in my office who I told you about in earlier pages. Next time you feel that you have made the most amazing pitch, a world beater, that on any other given day would earn you enough commission to help you afford a brand new car, and the prospect turns you down - do not despair! For all you know, your prospect's husband could have just walked out on her, or she could have been involved in a minor car crash that morning, or could have other personal issues you just are not aware of! It is rare as humans that we run perfectly and to 100% all of the time. How many times have you turned down the chance to go out for dinner because at that very moment you 'did not feel like it' only to regret it when the day of the meal comes around. Or what about the other way around? If you are like me, create plans so extravagant and exciting when you are in a super good mood only to wish you had kept your mouth shut on the day of the plans?! The same thing can happen to your prospect; their mood can affect what state of mind they are in when they see you.

When we deal with someone who is dealing with negative emotions such as fear, worry, sadness or even anger at the time of your pitch a person's emotional defences could be raised up to scare away a predator. We both know you are not a predator, however in a certain state of mind a person can see you as this. People can be scared due to past experiences with sales people who have ripped them off before. Maybe they are scared about making a decision that could turn out to be a bad one or will be looked down on as being a wrong decision by their peers. Perhaps your prospect is worried about your company's ability to fulfil the order on time as they have read one or two negative reviews online. Maybe they are sad because their daughter's beloved goldfish died that morning and they had to explain to the youngster about death and the afterlife. You do not know about these underlying factors that may be holding the customer back and can put you on the back foot, however learning to recognise these emotions in the buyer will give you the chance to either adapt your pitch, or ideally you can to try to reschedule the meeting.

If you encounter a prospect who appears to be high on life and ecstatic as hell - make the sale there and then!!! Positive energy is your friend!

Daniel Goleman wrote an absolute smasher of a book called Emotional Intelligence. In this book Daniel discusses EQ (Emotional Intelligence) and how at times it can mean more than IQ and be far more important in decision making. I urge every reader to study this book. The difference between a good sales professional and an awesome sales professional is their understanding of emotional intelligence. This works for the understanding and reading of your prospect or client but also your own emotional state too. If you can master your own emotions or at the very least understand them a little better then your sales will go through the roof.

Your Worst Enemy? You!

Are you behind on your credit card bills? Good! Pick up the phone and start dialling! - Jordan Belfort

There is an enemy inside of you that can harm your progress as a sales person. It can damage your potential not just in your career, but in your personal life too. It is a disease the lies amongst all of us. Something that can linger if not addressed can cause major harm. I am no saint; I suffer from this from time to time and even in writing this book it has battled with me on numerous occasions sometimes beating me on more occasions than I would like to admit!

What is this harming condition?

Procrastination.

Yeah, I am sure you have suffered from this. In fact, I am willing to put good money down that every reader of this book has suffered from it, and awareness of it is a great start to overcoming it.

The reason I bring this up is that procrastination can cause damaging consequences to your sales career; I have worked in sales offices where no work is done, or is done slowly due to procrastination and if the staff involved can overcome this they would absolutely smash their targets and be forced to create larger goals.

Put simply, procrastination is the art of of delaying or postponing something (Thank you dictionary.com!). What a way of putting it - 'the art'. It is an art I guess. I am sure if I asked you to write down the names of 3 people you know who have mastered this art it wouldn't take you long to write a list. These are the people that display amazing potential in anything they do and can clearly go on to do whatever they want to an amazing standard and yet due to what some people may call laziness they fail to reach their potential.

Maybe this is something in you that you can recognise. Have you ever found yourself just staring in to space with every intention to work and yet you can't just motivate yourself to do so. This includes housework too! How many times have you sat watching the TV just staring at adverts that mean nothing to you and yet despite how many times your wife has asked you, you just can't quite get off that sofa to take the rubbish out? Or perhaps instead of making that important sales call, you check your Facebook account for the 10th time that day just to see if your latest crush has updated his profile photo. Have you recognised that person in your office who would much rather talk to their colleagues about last night's football performance than to run their sales figures so they can set some effective targets?

Be honest with yourself right now - is this person you? Admitting so is not a bad thing; if you really want to increase your sales in the next 30 days, I encourage you to dig deep and admit these things now. Admitting so, and recognising the fact you procrastinate is the start of the battle and in doing so will allow you the chance to work on it and progress forward.

Now stop procrastinating and admit the fact you procrastinate!

It's funny, the solution to this issue is so easy as soon as you identify the reasons we procrastinate. To me, procrastination runs parallel to sales call reluctance. A book written by George W. Dudley and Shannon L. Goodson goes into amazing detail in to the psychology behind this invisible force, the attributes certain people carry and how to break through these barriers and I would really recommend dedicating some time to this book!

Let's go back several chapters and revise what I have said about goal setting. If you walk into a shop with no idea as to what you went in there for or what you need to get, then what is going to happen? The likelihood is one of three things; you will leave empty handed, you will leave with the wrong items, or you will leave with half the shop in bags and a maxed out credit card. Or picture a friend asking you to help tidy up their garden, and when you arrive the garden is an overgrown yard, not worked on for two years and seems like an endless task - where do you start?! As soon as you break the yard down into manageable goals and smaller tasks all of a sudden the task becomes easier and there is a clear defined end to the project. Procrastination can happen in us all when we have not set out a clear plan as to what we mean to achieve. Our minds have become programmed to switch off and find distraction when faced with tasks many of us would consider hard, boring and meaningless. Have you ever found yourself just watching one more episode of your favourite show before you do the washing up, or maybe just checked Twitter one more time before you called your prospect? I will be honest, I have been guilty so many times of the latter! Set your goals!!!! Having a clear defined goal will help you to break the task down and give you a clearly set beginning, middle and end.

So with the above theory, imagine right now you have a daily sales call list. This list is fairly easy; these calls are made to current customers so you aren't cold calling, and you already have relationships with these people, but your list has grown considerably recently. You have 35 names and numbers on the list and only short windows to call them in and so you know time is tight. Low and behold, your colleague has been called away and due to target deadlines looming, you take it upon yourself in your good nature to help them out. They have 22 calls on their list and you suddenly find yourself with 57 calls to make! What a nightmare. Normally when this type of task is put in front of us, we are prone to just stare at the list in disbelief thinking; "Where do I start?!" We look it up and down, scratch our heads whilst analysing the list just wondering what we are going to do. We start to waste time - we look through the list again, allow ourselves the chance to have another cup of coffee in the hope the caffeine hits us and gives us a new lease of life, and then we return to the list thinking "Where do I start?!" and then go on to whinge and moan about how our workloads have been doubled. Sound familiar? What a waste of time that was! Just imagine if this person had just set a plan, set a goal and did everything they could to smash that goal?! In this scenario, the goal is simple - complete the list. How do you achieve that? One call at a time. What more can you do? If your time is limited and your workload has increased, how can you avoid that workload if you can't delegate it, or ask for help? You can't. The only thing you can do is actually work, and get those calls completed!! Start from the top and work your way down!

One of my earliest mentors once told me to; "Read everything from top to bottom, left to right." In doing so, everything becomes clear and no mistakes can be made.

Sticking with the subjects of lists - let's discuss 'to do' lists. Yeah, I am sure you have one. I am currently staring at a Post-it-Note on my wall that says "Go to ToysrUs, Wash the Car, Write Christmas Cards, Iron!" To me, to do lists are an incredible tool - they reduce the load on my mind and just make me feel more relaxed so I can sit down, put my slippers on and read books like the old man I am! But how many of you can admit to doing the easy task first, and leaving the harder tasks last? What about your email inbox? Many of us use that as a sort of to do list. Do you ever find yourself going through the inbox, getting the easy tasks out the way first and then find there is always that one email containing a job that you know will take the most time and effort that seems to sit at the bottom of the inbox and always gets put back day after day? I want you to start to flip this idea on it's head - do the harder jobs first! Instead of allowing the tough task or the most time consuming job to sit around all week, frustrating you and playing on your mind, get it done now! I assure you that you will feel so much better for doing it. In a sales scenario - complete the more time consuming quote first, or put the tougher prospect at the top of your daily tasks (the only exemption from this rule is for those people who need to warm up a little and get in the swing of things before they make a tougher or maybe more important call. We all need warming up, and sometimes making a few easy follow up calls and maybe a service call may just get the mind and tongue working in sync).

The fear of rejection can cause many a good sales person to delay picking up the phone or going to knock on the 100th door of the day. As I mentioned in my chapter on rejection, my colleague whom had such a fear of rejection actually stopped doing his work and was a person who struggled with this. The greatest of us have had second thoughts about completing tasks or doing things over doubts and the fear we produce ourselves. You have to remember that fear is born deep within us! Fear is an emotion set up to protect us from external dangers. This of course can be a good thing - we are understandably scared of heights as our minds do not want us to slip and fall to our deaths! If you have been in relationships in which the other person has hurt you in any emotional or physical way, of course you are going to be scared about entering a new relationship in case you are to get hurt again. Fear is nothing to be ashamed of, and you should embrace it and understand it (this is where emotional intelligence can play a pivotal role in your development). If you do become fearful of something, someone or a certain situation it is simply your mind giving you those early warning signs and that is also another reason why we procrastinate - to distract us from this negative emotion. We distract ourselves, forget about the fear as we are no longer thinking about the fearful task and all of a sudden our emotions become balanced once again - until we remember about the task we have been putting off!

Everything you want is on the other side of fear - George Addair

For most of us, the only thing to truly get us past the fear of a task, is to just do it. Just take the leap, take the plunge and come out fighting. Once you are past that barrier, reward yourself, and keep on practising!

Back in 1987, Susan Jeffers had her first book published which you may have heard of! Feel the Fear and Do It Anyway is an award winning book and was the result of heartache for Susan; after divorcing her husband of 16 years, feeling sick and tired of heartache, Susan started to research relationships and this all led to her putting pen to paper. The journey wasn't easy however! She faced rejection after rejection from publishers however she never let go of hope and kept moving forward! Susan has 5 'Fear Truths' which break down many of her thoughts in to five bitesize chunks and 'Fear Truth 2' states;

"The only way to get rid of the fear of doing something is to go out and...do it!"

There you are! I am not the only one that believes we need to at times just jump in head first and get the job done.

So next time you are facing a sales call which you are put off by, for whatever reason just remember what Susan Jeffers says! Pick up that phone, write down what you want to obtain from that call, whether it be a face to face meeting or even a sale, and just do it!

Improve Your Personal Brand!

The reward of our work is not what we get, but what we become - Paulo Coelho

You know the old saying - "It's not what you know, its who you know". You've heard that right? I want you to forget that. Get it out of your vocabulary, it's old and dated. Replace that saying with; "It's not who you know, it's who wants to know you." Say it again; "It's not who you know, it's who wants to know you!"

A lot of our business occurs from recommendations. If we as sales professionals can create a profit for our clients, or provide them with the solution to the problem they have been struggling to find, they are more than likely going to recommend you to a friend, and even use you again (remember the Customer Cycle of Satisfaction?) Therefore we must always be the absolute best person we can be at all times and provide the best solutions in an ethical and honest manner. The more likeable you are as a person and more memorable, the more likely you will see repeat business.

Let me emphasise this point with the tale of two estate agents. Recently, I have been selling my first every property and went on to upsize. In selling my house, I picked out two Estate Agents from the local ads and booked them to come round, valuate my house and give me some options as to my next steps - to be honest when I first called them I wasn't too sure if I could even afford to move so it was a very simple exercise to just test the water and see what I could do. One Saturday morning, I booked these people in to see me an hour apart. The first agent, Andrew arrived on time, and appeared very presentable - he was well dressed and appeared very calm, and straight away started to build a relationship with me. I spoke with Andrew in great length about what kind of property I was looking to buy and Andrew kept asking me questions with regards to my ideal location, my ideal property and my tastes. Andrew, having noticed a photo of my Children on the wall asked me questions about them and went on to tell me how he had children the same age as mine and there was a relationship developing between us straight away. Andrew went on to take detailed photos of my house with a top of the range camera, took measurements and took all the details he needed there and then. During the whole visit he was never rushed, he was open and ensured that all of my needs as a customer were satisfied. Andrew left and I sat and waited for the other agent to arrive.

I waited. I waited some more. And then, yeah you guessed it, I waited some more.

Twenty minutes later than the appointment time, a lady arrived at my door (you see, I can't even remember her name!) she was flustered, which I guess was due to her poor time keeping, and rushed in to the house. She was there literally five minutes. There was little conversation; in fact, that's a lie. We did talk, but she was more eager to tell me about how she was going on holiday the next day, and was in "holiday mode" and didn't qualify me with any questions about my needs or what I needed. The next thing she did astonished me. She pulled out her iPhone, and took photos of the house. I could not believe it. I think she could see the amazement in my face and told me one of the team would back another day to take the photos with a better camera. After that had happened, we said our goodbyes and she left. However, this estate agency called me several days later to tell me another agent had to come round and finalise the details on the house, take photos and measure up. I had to ask a friend to hang out at mine as I didn't want to take time out of my career just for the estate agent to complete the half job they had already started. I later found out the lady who attended my house first time round is a Sales Manager for this agency! Shocking.

I am sure it is obvious who I went on to choose to sell my property.

As a customer, when meeting these sales people, I had to give my money, and allow commission to be given to the person whom I trusted the most. On this day I was confronted with in theory, two sales pitches. These people were put in front of me with the chance to sell my property and earn some commission for their troubles - but in theory, only one person turned up. As with my financial advisor Allan, I will more than likely use Andrew and the Agency he works for again in the future and I truly hope his sales career goes from strength to strength!

So what is it we should do to improve our self image? What is it that makes us more likeable to others? These are tough questions to answer and one thing I will say is that there are no real right or wrong answers. There are times when two people for whatever reason just will not see eye to eye or get on. Maybe not to those extremes, but two people may not have as much natural rapport as two other people and that is something you need to take note of and as with rejections, do not take it personally! If you cannot win the client or prospect over - hand him over to a colleague. Take a step back, and find someone who that person will work better with. Never force a relationship when one simply cannot be created. This will only cause more harm.

Our self image is defined by many things and not just our physical appearance. Of course, there are laws of attraction and our appearance does matter and we should do what we can to be at the top of the game. This isn't a vanity thing, unfortunately it is a fact of nature. Take two cats for example. You are outside your home, and two cats walk up to you from different angles. One is beautifully groomed with shiny, healthy fur. It's collar looks new, and he struts over to you with a self confident step. The other cat shuffles towards you. She looks flea ridden, her fur all scraggy and unclean with a collar which looks like it was bought 5 years ago. Who are you going to stroke first and pay the most attention to?

Maybe a bit of an extreme analogy, but the fact is that appearance does matter to the buyer. You do not have to be an Adonis, or a 'Miss World' candidate, but you need to look like you take pride in your appearance and take care of yourself. The appearance of someone who looks after themselves shows us one thing at the very least - they take care of themselves. If a person takes care of themselves, are they going to make an effort to take care of you? I would say yes.

So, what can you do to make sure your first impression counts?

- Iron your clothes!

Sounds simple I know, but I see this a lot. Especially in young sales professionals. A creased shirt winds me up. A decent iron costs £20, a board can set you back £12, and it takes 2 minutes to iron a shirt!

- Maintain your hair.

Once again this doesn't take long, but turning up to a sales pitch with bed hair just does not cut it.

- Wear perfume/aftershave

Do not over do it. You are not looking to drown your client in cheap smelling alcohol, but you need to have an air of authority about you.

- Dress for the occasion

You can never be overdressed. A sales professional who turns up wearing clothes that they are proud to wear will make them look like a success, and success attracts success!

- Smile!

How infectious is a good smile?! I was driving to a meeting earlier and as I was driving I saw a young lady walking along the side of the road with a bounce in her step and a smile on her face. I could not help but smile back! The more you smile, the more infectious and inspiring you will be. Even the physical motion of you smiling can release endorphins within your body that make you feel happy. So the next time you feel down in the dumps, just smile. Within 5 minutes you will have cheered up! And the next time you shake hands with a client, smile. It sets the tone for the rest of the meeting.

As I say, physical appearance is just a minuscule part of what I mean about personal branding, but be wary of these factors - I want you to increase your sales in the next 30 days and I am not going to leave anything to chance!

So, your brand. Your legacy. The reason people come to you for the best advice and for the best service in your area. This is defined by WHO YOU ARE. I would like you to write down 5 attributes that you believe other people see in you. Five things that if asked, your customers would say about you. Or maybe even your colleagues. Take some time to think about this, and write down the key five characteristics that describe you most;

1)_____

2)_____

3)_____

4)_____

5)_____

I am hoping in fact that this didn't take too much time. I am hoping that by now you are aware of who you are as a person and you understand what people see in you. There is no right and wrong answer to this. This is simply an exercise to get you to start to understand how others see you. I truly hope that no negative attributes sprung to your mind as to how to describe yourself. Listen, it is good to be honest, and if they did then you and I know it is time to change. The negative attributes that would concern me are;

Selfishness, greedy, self centred, egocentric, narcissist, arrogant, cocky, loud mouth, know it all etc.

These are all things we do not want to be known as if we want our sales careers to grow. If you are known as any of these, it is not too late to rebrand yourself. Of course, it takes time, but if you keep practicing and show good work you will loose these attributes and your personal brand will develop and grow.

Remember, your personal brand is your reputation and with the likes of social media now a massive part of our society, our personal branding means more than ever. Therefore, I keep saying this but I cannot get this point across any more - be the best person you can be!

I want to share with you a short story about how honesty and being completely transparent with a customer can reward you down the line. Andrew Peterson is the founder & CEO of Signal Sciences and during his college years he worked in retail sales at The North Face. Andrew describes how his favourite customer interactions were always the ones when he would recommend the customer go somewhere else. I can imagine many of you cringing at this, and I am positive there are many sales managers out there who would be wanting to get rid of Andrew from their team. But Andrew states he was always intent on getting the customer the best product for what they were looking for; "When that wasn't something from our company, I'd tell them what they should get instead and where to get them from…they always ended up buying at least something from me because they were so shocked I wasn't just pushing our products on them. A great lesson I learned from this is that the best salespeople are the ones you trust."

Do not be scared to self promote either. Some people see self promotion as a way to brag, show off and be arrogant about your achievements. If you are happy with your life, and your achievements in home life and also your career - share them! See your social media and even your real life as your CV. I personally set up a personal Twitter account to be used as a business platform. A way to contact customers and clients on a more personal level and for people to see me away from just the work environment. I keep this Twitter account as 90% work related, engaging in customer discussions, giving praise to the work they do, but the final 10% is to promote myself on a personal level so that those clients who only ever see me with my work head on understand what makes me tick and to have an insight to my personal life. This then helps me to build a personal relationship with my customers with ease and has made me far more approachable. In doing this I have aimed to make my name as the first point of contact for new customers and for also referrals. My mindset is that when people think of the company I work for, they then think of me second. I do not see this as a way to brag, I just want my company to do well and of course for my sales to continue to grow and I see myself as playing a key part in that.

What appeals to you when meeting someone new? What draws you to them? It is for these same reasons that your clients will come to you and see things in you that they like.

A good sense of humour is an incredible attribute to have. Being able to tell a joke, and being able to take a joke will make you an indispensable member of any team - either in the office, or during your sales pitch. Being able to make fun of yourself is by far one of the easiest ways to maintain humour, and this is such a safe option as to avoid offending any of your audience! If you are struggling with your humour, go to a couple of small comedy clubs and soak in the atmosphere. Watch several of your favourite comedian's stand up shows. Watch and learn how the comedian's timing is more important than the joke itself at times and incorporate that in to your sales pitches and phone calls. As I said before, avoid making your prospect the brunt of your joke otherwise you may as well take that commission cheque and put it in the shredder yourself! Learn the ways in which you can make yourself the target in your humour and you will lower many defences in your clients and make them much more relaxed. For example, poking fun at your own appearance is by far one of the easiest ice breakers in the world and can really make people feel at ease. Knowing you don't take yourself so seriously can give people around you a sense of calm and will start to lower their guard with you and allow you to start asking qualifying questions for their needs as a customer.

Don't forget that in all of this, your personal brand needs to mirror the brand of the company you are representing. You are a representative of this brand and you need to remember that you are in many ways the face of your business. Your business will have of course a mission statement (do you know yours?) and you need to be aware of this and be the image that your company needs you to be.

In my recent years of studying, I have found that those who give to others and help those around them actually turn out more successful and have way more come back to them than what they gave. When we give, the Universe returns back to us in greater numbers! To be seen as a kind hearted, helpful person too will do you absolute wonders when it comes to your personal brand - everyone wants to be associated with a loving, kind person and no one wants to be know Ebenezer Scrooge. You do not have to go out there and give all of your wages to charity, or donate all of your spare time volunteering at your local dog kennels, but ensuring that one of your goals in life is set to assist others is key. This can even be a part of a mentoring scheme for colleagues as I discussed earlier. Taking a young colleague out for lunch to help them in their work will mean the world to that individual and will cost you very little.

I have spoken about Tony Robbins a lot in this book. Quite frankly, he is a massive idol of mine and having read many of his publications I am proud to say that I have learnt a lot from him - not just in my career but in my private life too. You may know Tony as being a larger than life character whom over his years has accumulated massive fortunes, has a beautiful wife, lovely children with a work schedule so full he can afford large beach side mansions and all the better things in life many of us can only aim for. There is one story of Tony that has really stuck with me and I would like to share that with you. Tony's life wasn't always as flush as it is now and back in his 20's, he was living in a 400 square foot apartment and was down to his last $21 dollars. There was an all you can eat restaurant several miles away and thinking about 'stocking up' for Winter, Tony made the 3 mile walk to the restaurant. By his own admission, Tony could not even afford the money to drive there. Tony got to the restaurant, and started eating as much as he could, when he saw the door to the restaurant open and in walked a very attractive young lady. She of course caught Tony's eye and he of course looked to see who the lucky man was who was accompanying her - he was about four foot tall, around 8 years old and he was wearing a three piece suit and was quite obviously this lady's son. The little boy had opened the door for his mother and even pulled out the chair for her. Tony describes how this young man was so loving towards his Mum and how present he was in the moment. After Tony had finished his meal, he paid his bill and with his final $16 or so, he walked over to the table with the little boy and his Mum. He said to him, "Listen, I just want to tell you, you're a class act. I saw you hold the door for your lady, and how you pulled up the chair." The little boy responded; "Well she's my Mum!". Tony responded, "That's even more cool! And it's pretty cool you're taking her to lunch like this." The little boy said, "Well I'm not taking her to lunch, because I'm only eight. I don't have a job." Tony Robbins then smiled, and replied "Well, you are taking her to lunch," and he took every bit of change he had left and put it on the table in front of the little boy.

Without looking at the Mum, Tony left the restaurant, now not a penny to his name, and started to walk home. For many of us, we would start to experience a sense of panic, maybe a little bit of fear. Maybe the urge to go back inside and take the money back? But Tony didn't. In fact Tony describes this moment as "...the most free I had ever felt in my life."

The next day, Tony went to check his mail and inside was a cheque for $1200. This was from a friend whom he had lent the money to years ago and quite frankly had given up hope of ever seeing this money again.

The more you give away, the more you will get back - Wayne Dyer

So let's think about this some more. If you are truly a nice person and are willing to help others, then you should receive back in abundance. But think about how well your personal brand will grow should you market your achievements well. Remember self promotion is not bragging. If you are proud of your achievements then why not show them off? Companies all around you are proud of their charitable donations and are not afraid to broadcast them to the masses, so why shouldn't you? Find ways in which you can give back to your local schools, your local communities, or raise money on larger scales. It is so easy these days to get fundraising for any sort of good cause and there many websites out there that will help you raise funds.

Back in 2015, I set up a charitable bike ride to raise funds for a local charity which is close to my heart. The Reality Youth Project was set up in the same village as I was brought up in and I had a close relationship with the charity when I was in college. I decided to cycle the 165 miles from my village to Canterbury in one sitting in the hope of raising funds for the charity's latest project. Reality had just purchased a run down double decker bus and were looking to turn it into a mobile youth centre to allow young people the chance to socialise in a warm and safe environment with the latest games consoles, DJ decks and all sorts of gadgets. As I started planning, the team grew larger and there were five cyclists in total all willing to cycle with me. We also had a support team who followed in a mini bus in case we needed assistance. One drizzly day in May 2015, we set off from Canterbury with the target of returning to Leicestershire the same day. Unfortunately, 40 miles in to the ride, I suffered a horrendous crash. I lost control of my bike and at approximately 20mph I went flying over my handlebars and landed directly on to my left shoulder in a pile of dirt by the side of the road. The paramedics arrived and gave me a blissful dose of gas and air, and I had to go to Basildon Hospital for further treatment. It was there I discovered I had snapped my collar bone.

The rest of the team kept on going and didn't once think of giving up. After being discharged from the hospital, one of the charity team members collected me in their car and we caught up with the team and I was able to join the team in the support bus. Even with my arm in a sling, being quite high on pain killers, I joined the team in riding for the final half a mile to the finish line where we were greeted by all of our families, friends and we had a beautiful party to celebrate the achievement. That day, we raised just over £6000 for the charity which was put to good use on the double decker bus.

To this day, the bus is on the road most nights allowing young people the chance of spending time somewhere in a safe environment and is even hired out by schools and local councils during the day time for other events and projects.

To follow on this success, we completed the ride once again in 2016 - and I am pleased to say this time I actually paid attention to my riding and didn't fall off once! We raised a further £4000 on this ride and I have plans for more fund raising events in 2017.

For more information about this amazing charity, please visit;
realityyouthproject.co.uk

I found that after raising this money for the project, my personal reputation was boosted greatly. I of course am very proud of what we achieved that day which all started from my crazy idea of an endurance cycling event and even now a lot of my customers ask me about the bike ride and it has allowed various personal barriers to be broken down and friendships have been strengthened because of it.

Remember; your reputation is your brand. Your brand is your reputation. How are you known? How do you want to be known?

The Tennis Ball Theory

Don't find customers for your products, find products for your customers
- Seth Godin

Just roll with me on this one. This is something I picked up on by analysing and watching sales professionals in the field - not just in my own industry but also when I am out shopping. I am quite sad really, I love getting into conversations with sales people either on the phone or in person as I love to listen to their pitch and to see how well they are doing and to see if I can learn anything from them.

I remember one time, I was watching a sales professional in a shopping centre trying to sell the latest beauty product. I am not too sure what the product was, but I am sure it was some sort of natural seaweed hand cream. This man was approaching nearly every person that walked past him, which I did think was good - this guy was eager for a sale. However his body language and demeanour seemed very aggressive, to the point where many shopper's barriers were put up instantly. You could see that although there was a glimmer of intrigue in the prospect, due to the sales person literally forcing himself upon the customer, all of a sudden the customer would put up a barrier to protect themselves from spending money.

If you imagine somebody forcing their opinions on to you, what do you normally do? The stubborn child in us comes out and we stand our ground. We put barriers up, and do not listen to what has got be said. Even if the other person is right, the minute something is forced upon us, we put up a shield.

In sales, I call this the Buyer's Shield.

```
     Sales
     Pitch


  - - - - - - -


     Customer
```

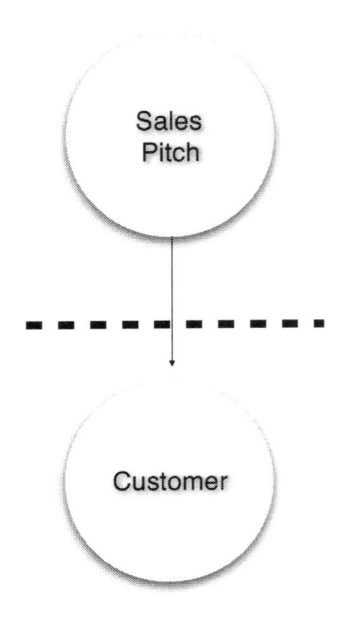

In this diagram, the Customer's Shield is illustrated by the dotted line. You will find, or may already know by experience that the harder the pitch and the more forceful you are, the stronger the shield becomes.

The shield can be put up for numerous reasons. Let's face it, we never like to buy something we simply do not need - but we do love to buy. Being forced to pay for something never makes anyone happy, we like to keep our money safe and to feel that sense of security that money brings to us.

So how do we get around this?

In a business to business scenario, a shield will still be out in place by the buyer however it will be much easier to take down. By qualifying your prospect and ensuring you are offering a product or service they actually need will make this easier. Gaining the trust of the prospect and building a relationship too will of course lower this shield (you know all of this!) No matter how much you plan and prepare, always expect a shield to be in place. People, no matter how large the company will have budgets to stick to. You will never expect to walk in to a pitch, say "hello" and have a sale just from that would you?!

The Customer Shield will always be tougher to break down when your sale is solely based on a personal level - in a retail setting, over the phone or in a chance meeting. In these settings you have little time for confidence building or to start a relationship, you have 5-10 seconds to make the right impression and to get that sale!

This is where my Tennis Ball Theory comes in to play!

Imagine sitting in a room with me right now. We are sat 10 metres away from each other, both facing one another. In my right hand, I have a tennis ball. Without warning, I throw it as hard as I can in your direction - what is your reaction? You will duck, dodge, flinch and try to not get hit by the ball, surely?! Of course you would! It's the same with any object - the harder I throw it at you, the more you will get out of the way of it!

Now let's take that same situation again. We are back in the same room, once again sitting 10 metres away from you. In my right hand is that exact same tennis ball. This time, instead of throwing the ball at you as hard as I can, I throw it in the air so that it starts to land next to you. When faced with this, many people will reach out and catch the ball as opposed to diving out of the way.

(I actually tried this in my office once, it was a great laugh! Give it a go! I cannot be held responsible for any damage though!!)

I want to make clear that I am not asking you to walk around your retail store and throw items in the air for your customers to catch them. This really is not my intention! This is a metaphor to be used within the creation of your sales pitch.

The first example relates to an over the top, overly forceful sales pitch. Without warning the item is pushed upon the prospect and their only reaction is to put up their shield and walk away (similar to a fight or flight reaction really).

The second reaction is that of an open pitch; not being overly forceful and allowing the customer the chance to say no. This may sound odd - we don't want the customer to say no do we? Of course not, but a no is a much better response to that in the first example. At least with a no, you can ask the right qualifying questions to see what it will take to get the prospect to turn into a customer.

The trick is to think of the Tennis Ball Theory when writing and rehearsing your sales pitch. Make life easy for yourself and try to reduce the chance of the Buyer's Shield from being raised.
Even in a retail setting, or in a one shot sale situation - you only have one chance to make the sale so you need to make it count. Don't scare away the client by ramming the product in their face!!

Let's go back several steps to my friend in the shopping centre. The one selling the fancy seaweed hand cream. Here we have a chap who is quite clearly an eager and ambitious sales person. He is asking every person that comes past him, but from what I could see he was asking the wrong questions. This professional was approaching prospects, with a bottle of the product and asking,
"Ladies, can I ask you a question?". My response to this kind of questions is to always say, "You just did ask me a question" and walk away.

Imagine the prospects being approached in this way. Put yourself in their shoes. You know instantly that this is a sales person trying to take your money and so your Customer Shield suddenly rises. You're tired from shopping all day, you want to go home and you want to save the rest of your money as you have spent enough as it is, and you walk away.

Let's use the Tennis Ball Theory in this professionals pitch.

My approach, would be to approach the prospect and ask the question, "I need your advice; which one of these two products smells better?" or maybe if I was using the Tennis Ball Theory properly I would say, "Here, catch!"

At least with this first question, you are doing two things. Firstly, you are gaining the customer's intrigue. Most people in this situation would like to help you, and you will then be given a much better chance to qualify the prospects and to develop a relationship. Secondly, this question is open and doesn't allow the customer to say no. A potential customer may say, "I do not have time." or "not today thank you" of which they have every right to, but even these answers will give you a much better chance of being able to qualify the prospect and seek out their needs. A simple 'no' response from the prospect will not allow this.

So take all of this on board. The harder you try to force someone to take a product or service, the harder the Customer's Shield will be to take down.

Try this technique in your next sales pitch and I assure you, shields will be a lot easier to take down.

Ripples In The Lake

The best marketing strategy ever: CARE - Gary Vaynerchuk

I wrote earlier about how the modern sales professional needs to change and adapt the way in which they sell their products. We are all taught, trained and raised to believe that the sales team are the finishers within a company. We are the people that close the sale, take all of the glory and take the praise. If we were in a football team, we would be the prolific strikers, finishing an incredible move and slotting the ball in to the back of the net in front of our adoring fans. If we were to carry on with the analogy, would the marketing team be our playmakers or our wingers, dazzling everyone with the awe inspiring skills to dribble the ball past everyone to then pass the ball in our direction and allow us the chance to strike?

That is by far, the most cringe worthy analogy I have ever had to write, but I think it illustrates a point doesn't it? I am sure you can see that stereotypical way of working in your line of work. A new product comes off your production line. It shines, glistens in the light and has everyone within your company talking. Who is it that then spreads the word of that product into the outside world? Your marketing team! They set about thinking of a whole new way to tell the World about how amazing your product is, why everyone should buy it and how it could change the way in which we all live! They use social media to get discussions going. They engage with their audience. They push for their campaign to go viral to spread their outreach until everyone knows about this product. Or perhaps the product is marketed towards specific markets, appearing in trade adverts or magazines reaching the decision makers that truly matter. Once this is all done and your market is inspired and primed for the product; the sales man steps in. Dressed smartly and ready to close, he enters the room with contract and pen in his hands ready for the proposed client to sign. He closes. Takes the glory and takes the praise!

That isn't the case in all lines of work or in all industries and I understand that; but I am sure you can relate to that as an example you have either witnessed first hand or have seen in society itself.

With all this being said, I believe you need to work more within the marketing department than you ever have in your career. Not only inputting your ideas and thoughts into the marketing process, but to also becoming an active marketer in the process.

Let's think back to a quote I mentioned earlier on in this book. Jules Marcoux talks about the "Growth Department" of a business; this is combining both the marketing and sales teams into what can only bring improvement and growth to the whole sales of a business. What if we were to look a little deeper in to this and were to class you as a marketer and a sales professional all in one? Think about it; you want your sales to grow, of course you do. This is what you do for a living, but the priming of a client is just as important as the close and neither one can exist without the other.

I was with friends recently talking about a new fundraising event for a local charity I am taking part in and we were discussing how we were to get the word out, and how to get people to become interested in the event without being too over the top and eventually boring our audience with it. This is where I mentioned my theory on The Ripple Effect.

I want you to visualise this next section, and please stick with me.

Picture yourself out in the open air. You're sat on the edge of a large lake. This lake is huge and expands out as far as you can see. As you sit at the edge of the water, you look around and see that the furthest piece of land away from you is around a kilometre or so away. You can see that the lake is in effect a large circle, cutting deep into monstrous grey mountains around you. There is no one else around you. The water is still; just lapping carefully around your feet. You put your hands on the dusty ground aside you and pick up a stone. The stone is no bigger than a 10p piece. You stand up, look back at the lake, and throw the stone as far out in to the water as possible. As it lands, ripples flow outwards from the impact until the strength is lost and the miniature waves die out. You take another stone, this time a little larger than the last. This one is the size of your mobile phone and weighs a little more. You throw it once again and this time when it makes impact, the ripples are larger and travel further. You reach down one last time and find the heaviest rock you can handle in one hand. You launch it as far as you can. The second it hits the water it creates a larger splash. The ripples and the waves now spread out further and quicker and reach a further distance but disrupts the natural stillness of the lake.

The lake is your market. The stones are your advertisements. The ripples are your impact.

Working in sales, you should recognise that buyers can so easily be put off by over the top campaigns in which information is stuffed down people's throats. This is represented by the largest rock - creating the largest waves and most disruption to the water.

To me, the key to marketing your product and also marketing yourself is to create little ripples first and foremost. If you were to throw a large rock in first you will only unsettle the market and disrupt people. It can cause people to put up their barriers and stop you from interacting with them. How many times have you signed up for a newsletter, or bought an item online and handed out your email out to a company. The more spam and junk emails you get the more frustrated you grow, surely? Although yes, the company is getting their name out there and keeping their brand in your mindset, however do you as a consumer want to keep having to delete emails or see their name pop up on you phone every time their latest offer hits your inbox? These are those big ripples that will only push a customer away.

Smaller ripples will keep your company, your brand and your product in peoples minds and keep them primed for that time you arrive to close, but will do it gently with out a large splash.

Let's head back to my conversation with friends earlier on in this chapter. As I explained to them the Ripple Effect, I introduced to them to how the Ripple Effect works on social media platforms. Let's imagine you updating a status or sending out a tweet as the same as you throwing a stone into the lake. As the information you send out hits the market (the lake) you send out ripples to potential buyers and prospects. Imagine one of your followers retweeting, or sharing this information as soon as they see it. This then creates a second set of ripples heading further out in to the marketplace, therefore reaching more potential customers. Then at the tip of this secondary ripple another 'share' occurs and the ripples head out even further. From that one tiny stone you threw you eventually managed to create enough ripples within the lake to create a tiny wave that came back and hit your bare feet back at the shore.

I am no expert in marketing and I can only share with you what I have learnt from studying, watching experts in the field and my experience as a consumer. However I am positive that the Ripple Effect can be seen as an effective way in which to spread the right word out to your audience without pushing people back and scaring them away.

Creativity is intelligence having fun - Albert Einstein

I advise you to think more about marketing in your day to day sales life. Social media plays a massive part in interacting to customers in today's sales world. I keep going on about this, however we all hold computers in our pockets which allow us to speak to customers where ever we are in the World and on any platform the customer wants to be contacted on. Social media plays an incredible part in our interactions in this World. I have customers whom I have never spoken with face to face, and have only spoken with on the phone a handful of times and yet we are constantly talking in the virtual World. I am sure you have customers similar to this or have acquaintances that you can relate this to. Whether you are reading this and are in charge of a large company who has millions of followers on various platforms of Social media or if you just manage your own personal account with several hundreds of followers; I am positive you can recognise how important it is to keep up to date in the virtual world and how our interactions can have massive impacts on our business and our sales down the line. Going back to the Ripple Effect, how many sales do you close or recommendations do you receive from customers who come across you on social media? Just recently, the company I work for gained the exclusive rights to retail a new food product in the UK. This product is very top end and comes with a hefty price tag for the size of the product but is the latest in modern gastronomy. Understanding the importance of this product, I uploaded as much information as I safely could on to my social media platforms and interacted with the manufacturers of this product and ensured I send out plenty of ripples out in to the marketplace.

Low and behold a couple of weeks later, a customer whom I have an incredible relationship with called me and asked if he could buy one of these items. I hadn't spoken to him directly about it before nor did he even know the price of the item. I asked him where he had heard about it, and his response was that he had seen my Tweets online and had done some research and was very excited to start using it.

This has the Ripple Effect written all over it. The first Tweet I had sent out was the first ripple. The more I Tweeted and the more I interacted, the further the ripples spread out across the marketplace. This caused so much excitement amongst our customers it was a case that the product ended up selling itself and I merely took the order.

That is the key to marketing isn't it. Excitement.

The most successful advertisement campaigns are created with excitement in mind. The more we can get our customers excited and turned on by a product or service, the more likely they are to buy!

We can extend that even further. We need to not only market our products, our company and our services, but ourselves too.

Those who stop marketing to save money are like those who stop a clock to save time - Henry Ford

Your personal brand should now be at the forefront of your mind and you should be proud of who you are. Remember, your personal brand is just an extension of you. You aren't putting on an act, this isn't a stage show with you as the star of the show. You now know what it takes to just be the best you can be and to be an overall nice person - and I want you to show that off. I want you to market the real you.

Listen, I have spoken before about how marketing yourself and your achievements can be seen as bragging but those who believe it to be bragging are merely jealous that they will never be as awesome as you are. So forget it and cut those people out of your lives. The more you market your good nature and the good work you do, the more you will appeal to a broader audience. You should never feel ashamed of the good things you do nor should you hide all the good things that happen in your life.

I feel like I have spoken about social media for a little too long in this chapter so I am going to extend this now to the real world. Real life conversations and interactions still matter even in this day and age. Never feel scared to talk to your colleagues, your friends or even family about how well you are succeeding, or feel shy to talk about the incredible charity event you took part in raising thousands of pounds in sponsorship money. Once again if you feel these people do not care or you feel that they are judging you then perhaps you need to address this and make changes to your choice of company. Those closest to you are put in place by yourself to care about you, to support you and for you to do the same back to them. If this isn't the case and you are always questioning their commitment to you - get rid of them!

Once again, you need to follow the simple rules of the Ripple Effect as to market yourself effectively. With just the same principal as your product, your marketing needs to be gentle and not over the top. The last thing your customers need, or your company needs, is you forcing yourself upon people and overloading them with information all about the amazing things you have done. This is where a bragging tendency can start to show and this will only damage your personal brand which will then have in turn a negative effect on your future sales.

The values of the World we inhabit and the people we surround ourselves with have a profound effect on who we are - Malcolm Gladwell

My old music teachers used to tell me that timing is key.

Isn't that true for everything in life? The time in which we think and the time in which we act are so crucial to every failure and every success we create. This can be the meeting of a spouse, or an introduction to a new friend, or even a new business venture or an idea for an invention. The time in which we act and set ourselves into gear are crucial to obtaining what we deserve.

This cannot be truer for any industry than the sales world and also the marketing world. The best sales people I have ever learnt from have all told me one thing; to keep our eyes open at all times. There are opportunities everywhere we turn and chances to sell are available to us at any time of the day. You just need to be aware of them. The more we interact with others and the more we interact with the World around us the more chance we have of creating more leads which will then give us a chance to market, and then close our sales.

Every person we come in to contact has the potential to become a customer in the future. Or, perhaps may recommend your services to someone else they know within their network. With this in mind you should never let your radars drop. Always be alert to those around you and pay attention to what is going on in the world, either in the virtual world of social media or even in the real world. Just a simple conversation in a pub or at your children's school gates with another parent can lead to much more down the line. This is what separates good sales people to great sales people.

Even if you aren't a sales professional and have a whole other career but want other opportunities to make themselves known to you. Opportunities in life aren't just going to walk over and slap you in the face. The more people you know and the more you network the greater chance you have of getting what you deserve in life. Imagine striking up a conversation with a random stranger only to become close friends with them down the line, and then from that they offer you more work or know of someone else that is hiring which then can offer you things in your career you currently aren't getting. The more people you know and the more you network yourself the better chance you have of your marketing ripples to reach out.

It's not just keeping your eyes open for people either. It is a case of listening to those around you, either people you know or people you don't and hunting down new opportunities. People will normally talk about their problems more so than their successes, this is just the way we are designed. Listen to what is being told to you, look out for issues that occur either in your local community or even in a prospect's work place - then use your problem solving skills to open up a conversation and try to find a solution to that problem! So many of us will shut ourselves off from the World around us and not pay attention to opportunities that are being presented to us.

Let's take a look a back at the example of me selling my house. The sale was in the final stages and the sold sign had appeared outside of my door. Low and behold, several days after the sold notice appeared, a flyer was posted through my door. The flyer advertised a professional packing and moving service. I was so impressed at the thoughtfulness of this I have kept the flyer and have it in front of me as I write this. Although it is a printed card, my address is hand written (something I always prefer over printed writing) and details the services the company offers. This family run business have recognised my problem, or the problem that will soon occur. I as a customer will need to move large amounts of furniture from one location to another. These guys are providing me with the solution way before even I had recognised the problem. They thought about my needs as a customer way before I had even understood my own needs. Now, who do you think is the first company on my mind when I think of house moving haulage firms?

The best marketing doesn't feel like marketing - Tom Fishburne

Your job as a sales professional is not just to close the deal anymore. You have a much stronger part to play in the whole sales process. Get involved with the marketing team and learn about what you can do to create ripples amongst your market place. Whether this be sending out promotional material to a database of customers you have set up yourself or organising the printing of flyers that your company have approved and sending them out as far a field as possible. The more ripples you send out and the more you prime your customers the easier the close shall be. Don't forget also your personal brand! You need to get yourself out there and network yourself!

Take a look at American real estate agents; they take out adverts on public benches and produce all sorts of promotional material which promotes them personally! They promote themselves more so than they do the agency they work for. Why? Because they know that it is them personally which draws people in. They know they have what it takes to develop strong relationships with their customers which will only lead to truly amazing things in the future.

Your Competition Can Be Your Ally!

Without competition, how can there be a winner? - Rob Spence

Pepsi v Coca Cola. PC v Mac. Mcdonalds v Burger King.

No matter what industry you work in, you are surrounded by competition. Other businesses similar to yourselves whom offer similar products or services at your same standard. There is no escaping competition and you should never think you are going to get rid of the competition. Even if you did, it would not take long for another business to crop up and start competing against you!

So how do we cope with competition, and how can the mention of competition from a prospect affect our sales pitches and potentially destroy our chances of signing the deal? Greater than this, how can we then turn our fortunes on our head and come out victorious?

First things first; I never want to hear you bitch, moan or speak badly about your competition. Go and re read my chapter on personal branding. How damaging for your personal brand could it be if you were heard attacking a competitor by a prospect?! Doing this would make you look very dishonest and untrustworthy. I can imagine there may be some banter amongst your colleagues regarding the competition behind closed doors and I would suggest it is good practice not getting involved in this. These kind of discussions are just negative and will not only fill your mind with negative comments and thoughts but will also make you store that information deep down in your mind. The more you stay away from these discussions, the less chance there is of you repeating some of these terms when out in the field. Hearing one person put down another competitor really puts me off, not just as a colleague but as a customer too. If you feel you need to lower another hard working business down, then you are not working hard enough to raise yourself above them.

If you do find yourself being beaten by competition, you need to ask the question; Why?! If you have followed my advice, your relationships with your customers will be on point and this at times will take away any question of competition - brand loyalty kicks in to play here. In my previous chapters I have talked to you about how a customer will more than likely stick with you, and your advice and you will find that this discredits competition. Relationships will beat competitive discounting and price wars 90% of the time. This is why your ability to build relationships, and also setting your personal brand is so important if you want to increase your sales in the next 30 days!

Building your relationships, maintaining them and allowing your personal brand to show through will help to smash your competition out of the water!

If you do ever find yourself in a battle with your competition, taking yourself above their level will help you to not only battle head to head, but will help you to win!

If some form of battle is about to start with a competitor, you need to prepare. This is where your research, planning and preparation becomes key! Address your own values when it comes to battles such as this. I can assure you, that when two, or maybe more sales people are competing for the same contract then your competition are battling for it harder than you. This does not mean you should sit down and let this happen! If you feel this happening, if you feel yourself procrastinating go back to your goals and remember why you are battling! If you want to own a larger house - get fighting for it! If you want a pay rise - get fighting for it! If you want to treat your family to the best holiday you have ever had - get fighting. Remember your values. Let's say tomorrow you have a big pitch and you are competing against 3 other companies, do you think these other sales professionals are watching yet another repeat of Friends, or trying to level up on Fifa 17??! NO! They are researching, and they are perfecting their pitch. They are doing everything they can to beat you. Yes, that's right. They are trying to keep you from your goals! What are you going to do about?

If you learn from defeat, you haven't really lost - Zig Ziglar

Remember that there will always be competition, that's just the way it is! So make sure you work damn harder than them and you will come out on top. Research your customers, research their goals, learn what makes them tick. What is your prospect's mission statement? How are you going to develop that relationship with them? Do they have a family? Where do they like to go on holiday? What is their favourite hobby? Who is their favourite Rugby team? It is these smaller details that will not only put your foot in the door, but will also allow you to walk in, and sit at the dining room table with them.

Look at the efforts Bud Fox went through to finally meet Gordon Gekko in the 80's classic movie Wall Street. Bud, a young Stock Broker called the offices of Gekko "59 days in a row", and then on Gekko's birthday arrived at his office, bright and early in the morning with a gift in hand.

If you truly want the sale - get up and start working for it!

Whilst we are on the subject of competition, don't be so stubborn and stuck up that you feel you can't learn from the companies you call your competitors. Many people I have come in to contact with stick their nose up at their competition at just the slightest mention of their name. I laugh when people call them 'The Enemy'. Yes, I have just been ranting about how you should fight your competition, but that is so that you win the sale. I want you to increase your sales in the next 30 days - it is in my best interests that you do and I want what is best for you! But do think about the things you can learn from these guys and girls who probably sell the exact same products or offer the same services as you. The reason you know this competitors name is because they are successful and with anyone's success comes a great deal of knowledge to learn from. Don't be scared to tap in to this resource and take from them what you can. This isn't about 'going behind enemy lines' and doing some stealthy reconnaissance - this isn't World War 3! This is about being humble enough to accept the fact your competition has in the past done well and you want to take as much knowledge and experience from them so that you can better yourself and become the greatest sales professional you can.

Price won't always be enough for you to seal the deal. Remember what I said in the earlier pages; relationships and brand loyalty will trump price 90% of the time! We are taught that price matters to everything, but to me there are times when you cannot discount quality. Be bold enough to be able to state this either. How many times have you heard the comment, "is that your best price?". Do you find that question utterly bizarre and quite laughable really. This just screams out to me the fact that the buyer doesn't trust you! I hate little price wars that go on and I try to avoid them at all costs. I am a very honest chap, and I would never rip anyone off. What is the point of me offering you a product at £X amount when I know really I can offer you it at £X - 10%. It makes no sense. I am more of a fan of setting a fair price and sticking with it. My normal reaction to this question goes a little like this;

"Yes that is the best price. I would not want to discount this product as I it would only harm the reputation and quality of the item"

After that I remain quiet and allow the customer to speak first. Give it a go. Next time you are asked if your service is the best price, speak those words above and then remain quiet. I assure you that the customer will not haggle any further.

You may be sucked in to a pricing war when it comes to two products that are identical, in fact the same, but your customer can sell theirs at £10 and you are selling yours at £15. These things do happen and happen quite often to me and the industry I work in - so how do you battle against this?

Follow my steps above on relationship building and this will be a rarity! Customers will not question price if they are buying from someone they trust and someone they know can deliver time after time. This adds much needed value to the product way before any discount is ever given.

What else can you add to that product to make it worth the extra cash? I am not talking about throwing a cuddly toy into the deal just to make it seem better and more attractive. But why should the customer spend their money with you? This is where your problem solving skills come in to play and you must think about everything your company and YOU stand for. Once again let's go back to that example of two identical products; let's use a set of 4 mugs (first thing I saw in my room as I wrote this). Your competitor sells four mugs for £10, where as you sell the exact same set for £15. Why should the customer buy from you if they can save £5 and buy elsewhere? This is the moment you need to add value to your set of mugs. Are you able to deliver before your competitor? Are you able to guarantee safe transport? Do you offer a guarantee? Maybe a warranty? When buying from you, does your company donate a percentage of profits to a charity? Maybe you are open to refunds, and your competitor isn't. Maybe your competitor's price is just a promotional price and after, their mug set returns to £17. There are endless examples in which you can hunt down that will add value to your product over your competitors which with the right research and planning you will be able to recognise and be bold enough to state to your buyer. Having a strong relationship with the customer will encourage them to buy from you of course.

Fig A

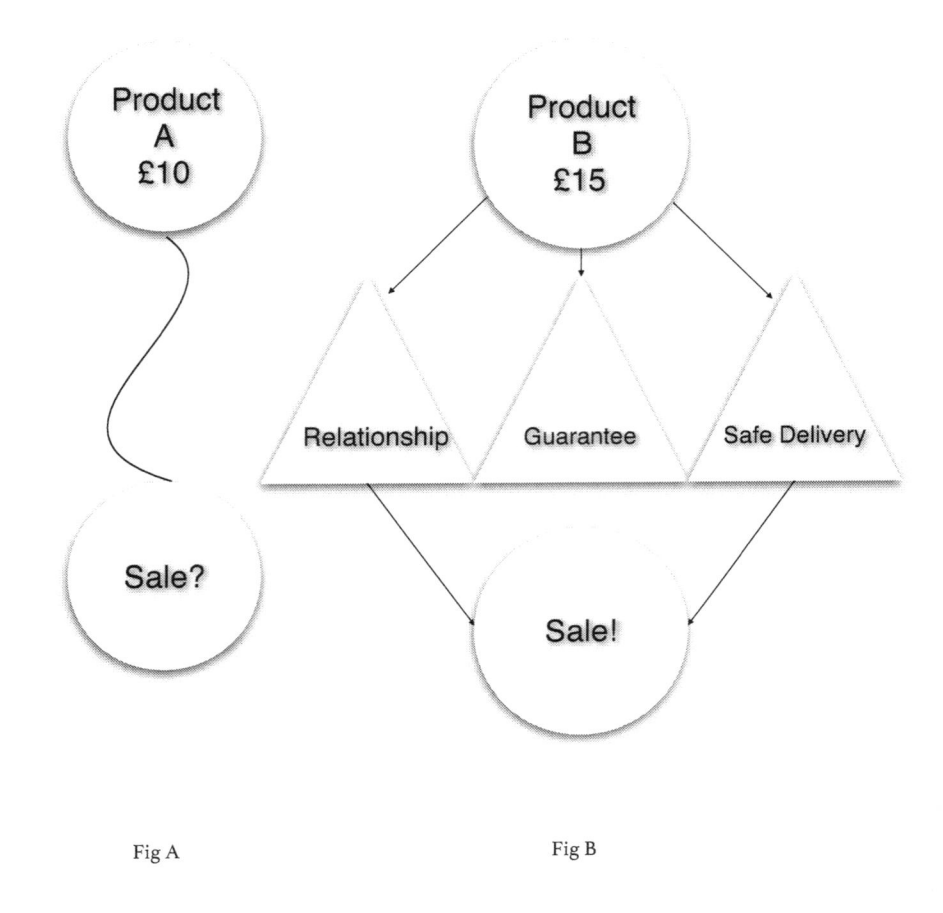

Fig B

You will never dispose of your competition and even if you do it will only be temporary whilst a new competitor gathers strength. Do what YOU can do! Work harder than those around you, research more, study more and never be scared to learn from the competition - you will be surprised what you can learn!

Fig A; Depicts a 'discounted sale'. Yes, the item is cheaper, but there is uncertainty.
Fig B; Depicts a 'value added' sale. Although more expensive, the customer is aware of the extra value added to the product.

You Made The Sale? Don't Quit Just Yet!

In the sales profession, the real work begins after the sale is made - Brian Tracy

Throughout my whole sales career, I have lived by one simple rule.

Sales = Customer Service.
Customer Service = Sales.

Or as I like to illustrate it as;

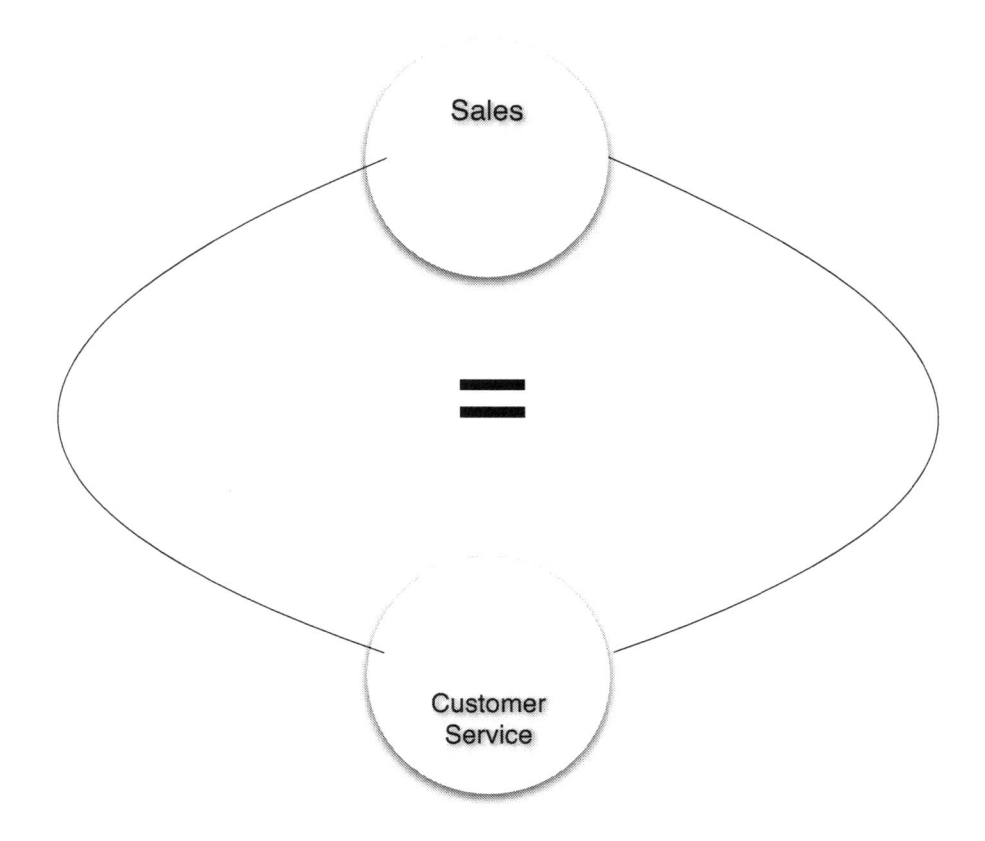

```
        Sales
          =
    Customer Service
```

My whole theory on sales is based around the fact that the nicest guys in the industry always come out on top. Yes there may be some amazing sales professional out there who using the best mind tricks and manipulation can sign a contract for a year long service or sell a product earning £1000's in commission, but that will just be a one off. Just think about when this customer finally comes to their senses and develops buyers remorse - are they going to recommend this sleazy sales professional to their friends? Are they likely to use this sales person again for advice? Of course not! Remember the Customer Cycle of Satisfaction mentioned in earlier chapters? Go and revisit it right now. The only way to keep earning a commission is to be the best person you can be, to open up and maintain relationships and to ensure your personal brand is always intact - this is how you make a living.

Many professionals have the misconception that as soon as the sale is made, their job is done. They are free to move on to the next prospect and carry along a cycle of prospecting and closing with no second thought at all to the people whom have bought from them. Remember our customers are those that pay our wages! It's not our bosses! Without customers, how do our bosses get money? Our salaries and our commissions are put together by our customers so why would you ever think of mistreating them?

I encourage all of my staff to always say 'thank you' after every sale. It takes a millisecond to do and goes a long way. Have you ever walked out of a shop, held the door open for someone and they waltz by without even a thank you - how frustrating is that?! A simple thank you can go such a long way and should be used at all times. However don't be afraid to go the extra mile either! A thank you letter, a shout out on social media or gifts will help you to solidify your relationship even greater and should never be over looked. What greater way to say thank you to a customer, than by buying them two tickets to the next home game of the football team they support (I mention 2 tickets - one for you and one for the customer. What a perfect way to solidify your relationship than escorting your customer on a paid for day out?!)

A thank you will always then lead to a follow up call. This is a simple way to ensuring that the item has been delivered safely and timely or that the installation of their latest machinery was completed to the high standards you promised. You may already know this information, but engaging your customers will show that you care. And that's where the true success comes for people in our trade; people who care come out on top. Following up with a customer will show that you care, and you can go to see your success in action. Keeping your name and your brand in your customer's mind will only do wonders for you - either via more business, or through referrals.

Following up too allows you the amazing chance to ask for feedback! Without feedback on anything in life, how do we know where we can improve? We can always improve either in our personal lives or in our careers and seeking feedback will help you to do that. Feedback will be given to you if you ask for it, and sometimes even if you don't and the best people to ask are your customers. Of course, your colleagues and your bosses will be a great source of feedback but surely the people who know how well you worked, or maybe how poorly you worked are your customers. Feedback need not be a massive life changing event either; sometimes the smallest feedback handed to you can add up to the greatest results. Take Toyota for example and their implementation of the Japanese word Kaizen, which means the process of finding and improving small problems. As a car company nearly 40 years ago Toyota went from a middle of the road (no pun intended) car company to one of the largest car makers in the World. No matter what position any Toyota employee is, they are all instructed to look out for small problems and even hold the authority to halt the production like if a problem is spotted. It is estimated that Toyota implement around a thousand tiny fixes in all of it's assembly lines. These changes can be anything from moving a parts bin by just a foot for example. One manager whom joined the company, James Wiseman had to complete a report and found himself hunting down all of the positives points that his team demonstrated and by his own admission bragged a little in his notes about how well his team were performing. He sat down with Fuji Cho (who is now the chairman of Toyota Worldwide) afterwards and he said, "Jim-san. We all know you are a good manager, otherwise we would not have hired you. But please talk to us about your problems so we can all work on them together."

You see, if you do not seek feedback how do you know how well you are doing and more importantly how can you improve for your next prospect? Perhaps your sales pitch could be worked on; is it too long, too short, with not enough information or not enough humour? Could your delivery times be improved, or maybe the way you came across on the phone could be improved. Do not take any of this feedback too personally. As with a sales call rejection, you seeking feedback WILL make you a greater sales professional which will only bring you closer to achieving your goals (if your goals are financially based) .

I am never sure why, but professionals I have worked with are awfully scared about asking for referrals. Referrals are key to making more sales in the future. In fact, you can organise your referral questioning earlier on your pitch and doesn't have to wait until the end of the sales process. What greater way to meet a prospect than by being introduced to them a trusted friend. A referral is worth 100% more than your initial sale so do not be afraid to ask for them. Every referral can lead to a further 10 referrals, followed on by a further 10 referrals from this initial 10. Within no time at all your prospect network is built up. And if you have followed my advice, your personal brand is so strong that these referrals may have already heard of you and have wanted to work with you for a while. Do you see how simple this whole cycle is? Approaching referrals need not be taxing and should not be an uncomfortable conversation. If you left your referral questioning for the time after your sale has been completed then I should imagine that your relationship with your customer is fairly solid. If this is the case just be bold and ask for the referral - what is the worst that will happen? The customer says, "No sorry, I just can't think of anyone" or "Sorry, I wouldn't like to share that information". But what about the best case scenario; your customer pulls out his address book and says "Here. You have done so well for me and my business network does need to know about you. Please photocopy every page in this address book and tell them I gave you their number," or perhaps your customer even phones the referrals herself and works as an opener on your behalf. If you do not ask, you do not receive!

Some sales professionals have been willing and open to take existing customers to their prospecting calls to meet new potential customers and what an incredible idea this is. What better advertisement for your services than to have someone sat beside you who knows how you work, and the incredible work you can do. This customer sidekick can also be proof that you follow through on your word and you are not just in the business to make a quick commission and that you offer the best services on the market. Perhaps this seems a little far fetched and a little out of reach for the work you do; however using testimonies from your customers can work wonders for you and in fact will sell your product or service much better than you ever could. Every online website you buy from has a review service, this runs from hotel bookings, holiday bookings, and even feedback on the smallest of gadgets that cost a mere couple of pounds. How useful are these bits of feedback to you when you are buying something. Knowing that someone before you has paid for, tried, and tested the product before you puts an awful amount of faith within you to trust what you are spending your money on. This will work in exactly the same way for you and your selling. Remember I do not believe in bragging but I do believe in self promotion. If someone is willing to give you a testimony then take it with both arms wide open. Get the testimony written down so that there is hard evidence that you can then republish on your social media accounts, your websites, newsletters or anything that goes out to customers. Whenever a customer is worried or facing some sort of trust hurdle to overcome to close the deal with you, a testimony can set in stone a new found trust which will allow you to close the sale.

> *Loyal Customers, they don't just come back, they don't simply recommend you, they insist that their friends do business with you - Chip Bell*

A sale continues long after the sale has actually been closed. The hard work has just begun. Customer retention is more cost effective than chasing new customers and can lead to much bigger and greater things for you, your business and the goals you have set.

Final Thoughts

You miss 100% of the shots you never take - Michael Jordan

I am a sales professional that is still learning and seeking feedback on my ways of working. I strive for excellence, always have, and in this trade I have found the ability to continue studying on a daily basis. I practice what I preach and everything in this book has been written from experience, from listening to my mentors and from studying books written by some of the leading sales professionals to grace this Earth.

In reading this book I hope that I have passed on to you some new practices that you feel you could put into place, or perhaps you have had a chance to revise material that you have heard about before or maybe experience in your day to day life. I believe that you are never too old to learn, and never too young to teach - and this is not just an age based saying to me. This is an experience saying. There are people in our trade whom have been in this business for decades who can still learn and adapt to new ways of thinking, just as a professional two weeks in to a sales career can learn from those with more experience.

We live in a beautiful World in which we are surrounded by knowledge which can be brought out and used if we simply ask for it. In writing this book I have learnt a lot about myself and the practises I use in my work and I feel I have grown because of my writing. I truly hope that even if there is just one passage in this book that you can take away and create more commission then I feel I will have done what I have set out to do.

You see, we all have stories to share and knowledge to pass on and that is something I want to encourage. The more we share and the more we help each other the more successful we can become and the more ethical our trade can be.

I hope that I can be your mentor, or perhaps there are things you would like to share with me. If that is the case please head over to robertspence.co.uk and get in touch. There is so much out there left for me to learn and I would love to sit down one evening and talk with you. Also, if you feel there is more you can learn from me, get in touch.

I made a bold statement in this book. A statement that suggested I can boost your sales within 30 days. I want you to tell me how you got on. Did you boost your sales? Good - get in touch and let me know. Did your sales plateau or even drop off? Get in touch. I want to know this feedback and I want to see what further help I can give.

In the final few pages I have set out a 30 day challenge - day by day. The more you put in to this, the more your sales will increase. Read through the challenge and then implement the ideas. Do not rush ahead, do not get ahead of yourself. Complete each day as it comes and put 100% effort into it. This will only work if you dedicate yourself to the program. If you just skim the surface, and do the bare minimum you will get nowhere. But if you dive in head first and give this everything you have then I assure you, your sales will increase within 30 days. If you can do this in the 30 days, I am positive that the following month, 6 months, year will be the most profitable you have ever had in your career.

Thank you so much for sharing this journey with me.

Robert Spence

Your Next 30 Days

Our greatest weakness lies in giving up. The most certain way to succeed is always to try just one more time - Thomas Edison

Every single stage of this challenge has already been outlined in this entire book, and I urge you to not partake in the challenge if you have not studied this book in detail. The next 30 days are going to be tough, but this is just the start. There will be no point in working hard for the next 30 days if you you are just going to quit straight after. Or even worse, there is no point in starting if you are going to quit mid-way through. I am not in anyway trying to put you off from starting, however I just want you to be the greatest sales professional you can be. This is going to take hard work, rejection and plenty of barriers to break through but I am certain that you will achieve amazing things from this. Just in buying this book, let alone reading to this stage proves to me how dedicated you are to bettering yourself - so let's get our heads together and smash this out!

For some of the days, you will need to concentrate on your goals. I need one of your goals to be; "I will increase my sales by 10% within the next 30 days". I need you to write this down, put it somewhere prominent and believe it. I want you to visualise yourself on a daily basis getting in touch with me to state your sales have increased. I am positive that in doing this, I will hear from you with great news!

Everyone of these daily tasks will be your focus for that day, however I still need you to go to work every day with your head held high, knowing that you are going to succeed. I want you to work hard, stop procrastinating and visualise yourself making a sale in every call you make or every visit you make. Work so hard that when you get home, you have a sense of pride knowing that you could not have put any more effort in to your day!

Day One

Write down three goals you aim to achieve within the next year. These can be about your finances, your family life, your relationships, your career or an adventure of some sort.

Once you have written down these goals, I would like you to include the goal "I will increase my sales by 10% within the next 30 days"

Take these goals and stick them somewhere you are going to see them on a daily basis. Your bedside table, the inner door of your wardrobe, your bathroom mirror maybe? Find somewhere you will see, and get used to reading them several times a day.

Day Two

Write down three people you would love to work with as your mentors. These can be people in your field or people you look up to and find inspirational. Alongside their name, write down why you have chosen them. What do you aim to learn from them?

Day Three

Take the name of the first mentor in your list. Call them and arrange a meeting. You don't have to meet them this same day, just get something booked in.

Day Four

Take your written list of goals and spend ten minutes creating a mood board. If you have set goals containing materialistic goods, print off photos of the goods you are going to get. For example if your goal is to own a new house within the next 12 months, print off an image of the house style you would love to make a home. Or if it is to go to Santorini, print off a photo of the beautiful landscape. Put this new board up, and spend 10 minutes visualising yourself achieving each of these goals. Find somewhere quiet, turn off your phone and stop all distractions. Picture yourself overcoming all of the challenges you can foresee and use your mind to see yourself achieving everything you are setting out to achieve.

Day Five

Find out who your leading competitor is within your industry and research everything you can about them. Who is their Managing Director? What year were they founded? Who by? Spend a good hour learning everything you can about them. Is there anything that this competitor does that you can adapt in to your own way of working?

Day Six

Spend time with loved ones. Your work life will only be successful if you remember why you are working, and who you are working for. If you have children, spend as much quality time with them as you can. Spend time with your husband, or your wife. Maybe go to see elderly relatives. Turn your phone off and live in the moment.

Day Seven

Take time out. We all need a rest. Put this book down, forget about me waffling on for just one day and relax. You deserve it.

Day Eight

Go back to your goals mood board, study it and once again spend ten minutes visualising yourself achieving each of these goals!

Day Nine

Take out your list of mentors, and contact number 2 on the list. Arrange a meeting with them and get ready to learn whatever you can from them. Have you met up with mentor 1 yet? If so, write down everything you learnt from them and revisit what they taught you.

Day Ten

Find out who the leading sales person is in your company, and do all you can to research them and find out how they have become so successful. Make contact with them and ask them questions about their career. Give them praise and start a relationship. If the leading sales person within your company is you, then is it time to find somewhere new to work?

Day Eleven

Discover what product in your company sells the most, is considered the most profitable and is the most popular. This can be a service package of some sorts too. Find out what it is and learn everything you can about it. Why is it so popular? Why do customers love it? How does it compare to other products you have to offer? Learn every little detail you can about it to the point you are confident you can answer any question that would ever be asked about it.

Day Twelve

Take your sales pitch, presentation or telephone script, set up a camera and film yourself presenting to an imaginary prospect. This is where many people cringe; get over it. You want to smash your goals right?! You can use your phone to film you, no one else has to be in the room. Go through your whole pitch as if you are truly going for a sale. Watch the pitch back and give yourself feedback. Would you honestly buy from you? Was your pitch boring? Can anything be improved? Work on what you feel needs working on, then go through the whole process again. Do this until your pitch is so flawless you are willing to take out your credit card and are willing to buy buy buy!!

Day Thirteen

Start to consider your personal brand. Who are you? What do you represent? How do you want people to know you? Put all of these thoughts on paper and start to implement these characteristics and start to become aware as to the consequences your actions have to your personal brand.

Day Fourteen

Take a day off again - put your mind at rest but just do one thing; make a charitable donation. This doesn't have to be a six figure cheque to a large charity but do something that can mean the world to another human being. Help an elderly neighbour take his rubbish out, or buy a toy for a friend's child. Today, aim to put a smile on someone's face. Make your donation as personal as possible.

Half Way Check!

Well done for getting this far! We are now half way through so well done for carrying on and doing everything you can. Do not let your efforts dwindle. Keep moving forward!

Keep getting in to your work day to day with the intention of increasing your sales! Keep making those sales calls, keep prospecting and keep being YOU!

Day Fifteen

Sit down with your goals and once again visualise yourself achieving each goal. This time I want you to introduce a close friend, a mentor or a loved one to your mood board. I want you to spend ten minutes showing them each goal, explaining why this goal means to much to you, and tell them step by step how you are going to achieve these goals.

Day Sixteen

Think about your personal brand once again and set up a social media account as a way to highlight this. Or, you could edit your current social media accounts to mirror your personal brand. Either way, focus on your personal brand and do everything you can to boost your image.

Day Seventeen

Who is your company's largest customer? Who are they and when did they start using you? Who is the sales professional who helped turn them from a prospect to a customer? Learn everything you can about this customer. When was the last time one of your team contacted them to say thank you? Is this something you can do?

Day Eighteen

Get in touch with your first ever customer and take them out for lunch. Show gratitude for the sale and also seek feedback on your performance as a sales professional. What did you do well? What could you do better if you were to complete this sale once again?

If you work in retail sales then spend ten minutes revisiting one of your first ever sales in your mind and try to give yourself feedback. Look for specific things you can improve on moving forward.

Day Nineteen

Offer to mentor a colleague, or someone you know outside of your company who is new to sales. Offer your time to them and do what you can to support this person. Also be willing to give them feedback on how they can improve. Make it your mission to see this person succeed.

<u>Day Twenty</u>

Write down your top ten customers, clients or even prospects. Find out who the decision makers are, and make the effort to find out an interesting fact about this person. Find out what date their birthday is. Find out how many children they have. Find out who their favourite football team is. Take all this information and write it down. Be willing to bring these things up then next time you have to call them.

Have you thought about sending them real birthday cards, in the post? (Yes, that still exists!)

<u>Day Twenty-one</u>

Once again, take time out with your family. Remember why you are working so hard. Treat your family to a meal out, or if the budget is tight, go for a picnic. Or even cook for them. Spend quality time with your loved ones.

<u>Day Twenty-Two</u>

Your goal mood board should now be second nature to you. You should understand every section of it in great detail, but once again take it down and study it. Spend 10 minutes visualising yourself achieving the goals and write down how you are going to do that! Do this before you go to sleep. Remember what I told you about how when we visualise our goals before we sleep, our subconscious mind will assist us in delivering what we deserve from life.

Day Twenty-Three

Seek feedback from people close to your business life. These can be your colleagues or even your bosses. Ask to spend half an hour with them, and ask them to tell you straight. What can you improve? How would your career improve if you changed certain parts of your work ethic? Take the feedback on board and think about how you can implement these changes.

Day Twenty-Four

Get in contact with mentor number 3, and set up a meeting with them. Revisit your notes on your meetings with Mentor 1 and mentor 2. Revise everything they told you and learn from them what you can.

Day Twenty-Five

Add another goal to your mood board. Make this one a charitable goal. Set yourself a challenge to complete in the next 12 months. Is there a cause you have been wanting to raise a lot of money for? Or maybe a cause you want to raise awareness for? Think about what you want to do, why you want to do it and plan out how you are going to achieve this.

Day Twenty-Six

Take time out once again. Turn your phone off and spend the day however you want to spend it. Enjoy!

Day Twenty-Seven

Once again record yourself making your sales pitch. Hopefully this time, it may need less work however do not think that it is perfect. Maybe show your pitch to your mentors - what do they think to it? How would they improve it?

Day Twenty-Eight

Aim to get rejected three times. Ok, not on purpose. But make so many prospecting calls that your chances of being rejected are increased. This may seem cruel and uncomfortable and that's what I aim it to be. The more you practice rejection, or at least how to handle rejection, the easier it will be. Besides, you may make the most amount of appointments you have ever made on this day!

Day Twenty-Nine

Nearly there! Remember the customer you researched earlier? The customer whom I described as your largest customer? I want you to call them and introduce yourself. Explain you are not calling to tread on any toes and that you are simply calling to introduce yourself and to give the customer another point of contact. Be clear with your name and give the decision maker your phone number. Start to build a strong relationship with this customer.

Day Thirty

For the final time during this 30 days, take your goals board and visualise each goal being achieved. How closer to them are you? How close are you to achieving these? Are you able to cross any off the list yet? If not, when will the first box be ticked? These may be year long goals but it doesn't mean you cannot tick them off early!

30 days have now passed - how did you get on? Be honest - have you put your full self in to this? I told you to dive in head first and I am confident you did. This whole book has been designed and written to give you the tools that have always been within you; sometimes they just need teasing out a little and that is the role I hope I have played. All of the tools you now possess need to be practised, rehearsed and refined. Like anything in life, as soon as we give up and stop doing the norm we start to drop our form and forget how to perform. This can also be said for when we create new habits and routines. To stop ourselves getting back in to old habits we need to practice the new habits and give ourselves praise for the times we do!

Contact me - did you see an increase in your sales over the past 30 days. Did you manage to record your stats? Have your commissions risen? Or have your sales targets been smashed much better than they normally have? Let me know! We can celebrate together! As your mentor, I will be very proud to know and I cannot thank you enough for allowing me to share this journey with you!

Head over to robertspence.co.uk and talk to me!

Acknowledgments

As we express our gratitude, we must never forget that the highest appreciation is not to utter words, but to live by them - John F. Kennedy

This is the part of the book I have been most nervous to write. There are so many people around me that have helped me, supported me and inspired me to write this book. Can I just say that if you are connected to me in anyway, if I have ever so much as smiled at you, you have made an impact on my life and I thank you for being there.

However a special thank you must be given to;

Mum and Phil, for putting up with my crazy ambitions and allowing me the chance to grow and develop. Thank you.

Dad, for being one of my first ever idols, and also for still being one of my most important mentors. Thank you.

Jacob and Alice, for being the two most incredible children a Father could ever ask for.

To Peter and Patrick, for giving me countless opportunities and taking your time to teach me all you know.

Victor, Patrick and Sean for guiding me and advising me through the crazy world of sales and business.

To every customer and client I have ever worked with, I cannot thank you enough for allowing me the chance to work alongside you.

To everyone that has ever doubted me, criticised me or ever knocked me down. My biggest thank you goes out to you.

Further Reading

An investment in knowledge pays the best interest - Benjamin Franklin

The Talent Code - Daniel Coyle

Counselling for Toads - Robert De Board

The Element - Ken Robinson

Be Bold and Win The Sale - Jeff Shore

How to Win Friends and Influence People - Dale Carnegie

Influence - Robert B. Cialdini

Emotional Intelligence - Daniel Goleman

Little Red Book Of Selling - Jeffrey Gitomer

Notes From a Friend - Anthony Robbins

The Game - Neil Strauss

robertspence.co.uk

Printed in Great Britain
by Amazon